# THE
# MAKING
# OF ME

December 2007.
from Ryan + Lisa. x

# THE
# MAKING
# OF ME

Finding my future after assault

# TEGAN WAGNER

**Pan Macmillan Australia**

First published 2007 in Macmillan by Pan Macmillan Australia Pty Limited
1 Market Street, Sydney

National Library of Australia
Cataloguing-in-Publication data:

Wagner, Tegan.
The making of me : finding my future after assault.

ISBN 9781405038232 (pbk.).

1. Wagner, Tegan.  2. Rape victims – Australia – Biography.
3. Rape – Australia.  4. Victims of crime – Australia –
Biography.  I. Title.

362.883092

Set in 12 pt Janson by Midland Typesetters, Australia
Printed in Australia by McPherson's Printing Group

Papers used by Pan Macmillan Australia Pty Ltd are natural, recyclable products made from wood grown in sustainable forests. The manufacturing processes conform to the environmental regulations of the country of origin.

*For my mum and dad,*
*Tracey and Noel Wagner*

# Contents

# 1

# My friend Kerry

THIS STORY BEGINS WITH Kerry. If it wasn't for my friendship with her, none of this would have happened.

Kerry and I were in the same class at school. We met for the first time in Year 7 at the school swimming carnival. We were both in the same sports team and she didn't seem to have many friends, so the two of us got chatting and we discovered that we had a mutual hatred of swimming carnivals. (I loved to swim, I just hated having to be in races.) Other girls probably would have swum in the races and put up with it, but me and Kerry were smarter than that. We thought we'd come up with a clever dodge so we could get out of racing entirely. I worked out we could keep the sports captains off our backs by running to the toilets every so often and ducking under the showers. That way we'd be wet and it'd look like we'd swum, even when we hadn't. This worked pretty well for a while, but then one of the teachers forced Kerry to go in one of the races, so she dived into the pool and faked a back injury. We played on that back injury for the rest of the day – Kerry couldn't possibly swim because her back hurt too much, and I couldn't swim either because I was helping her. By the end of the day we'd become firm friends, and we stayed friends, coming up with schemes and getting into mischief, right up until the night when everything changed.

Kerry wasn't like my other friends. She was always a bit of a wild girl, even in Year 7. She'd do stuff my other friends wouldn't dare to do. She would tell off teachers and be rude to people for the fun of it. She was the only friend I had who would poke fun at the popular girls, or play pranks on the kids who picked on us. We had in-jokes about other girls in our group and sometimes we'd spread rumours about them. We could be mean, but a girls' school is a pretty mean place. And we were never mean about each other.

Occasionally Kerry would cross the line and do something really naughty: once in Year 8 she came to school with vodka in a water bottle and she thought it was cool to drink it in class. My other friends and I couldn't believe it; we were like, 'Oh God, that's so *bad*!' But most of the time she didn't do anything too serious. She was naughty rather than bad – she was fun to be around. Me and Kerry were a team – she'd get us into trouble and then I'd talk us out of it again. The whole time I was at school, I didn't get detention once. I would do things like rock up with heavy make-up on, or create my own version of the school uniform. I never got myself into any trouble I couldn't talk myself out of – until the one time I did.

Me and Kerry had a lot of things in common. Her mum was a nurse, and so was mine. She didn't get along with her mum, and I didn't get on with mine. Her dad died of cancer, and so did mine. Basically we both came from pretty dysfunctional backgrounds, and that made us unusual at our school. Most of the other girls came from stable families where money wasn't a problem and everybody got along okay. Kerry and me came from a different world: we weren't poor, but we didn't have money to throw around. We weren't like the others, and it was one of the things that brought us together.

But there were differences between us too. I'd been brought up by my grandparents, although they treated me more like a daughter than a granddaughter. They were religious, and they were determined to give me a proper Catholic upbringing so I'd grow up knowing right from wrong. Life with my grandparents was ordered and predictable and safe. They were strict with me: they always knew where I was and what I was up to, so I could never get into too much trouble.

Kerry's home life was what mine *might* have been like if my grandparents hadn't been there to look after me. Kerry lived with her mum, and the two of them fought all the time. Kerry's mum wasn't the easiest person to get along with: she always seemed stressed, and she was one of the most pessimistic people I've ever met in my life. She believed Kerry loved her father more than she loved her, and there was always a lot of resentment between them because of it. She worked long hours as a nurse, and was often away doing night shifts, so she had very little idea of what Kerry was getting up to. Which was plenty, as we got older.

That was the main difference between me and Kerry. I had someone at home keeping an eye on me, making sure I wasn't getting up to anything too bad, but Kerry didn't. She was free to run wild. So she did.

THIS IS THE STORY of one night that changed my life forever. It began the way so many evenings do, with a couple of teenagers sneaking out. Most teenagers sneak out. Most kids take risks. It's part of growing up. And most of the time, you get away with it. How many girls have geared themselves up so they look nice, gone out to a party, and then started drinking heaps or taking drugs until they're not really thinking straight? And maybe some guy comes up to you on the dance floor and starts cracking onto you, and he's a bit creepy and you can't seem to get away from him. If you're lucky then one of your friends will come along and rescue you and you won't see him again and you'll go home perfectly safe and that creepy guy'll just be someone you joke about with your friends later: 'My God! Wasn't he a freak!' You had a narrow escape, but nothing actually happened, and it's all just part of the fun and you probably never even realise how close you actually came to something bad happening. But if you're *not* lucky, then that guy could drag you into the toilets or follow you out to the bus-stop and then a fun night can turn into the worst night of your life.

We've all been in the wrong place – doing bad stuff, hanging around bad people, trying stuff out. My story is about what can happen to you if you're in the wrong place at the wrong time.

# 2

# 14 June 2002

YOU KNOW THAT ONE friend you've got that your parents
hate? And the fact that your parents disapprove of them
just makes you like them even more? That was Kerry.
My grandparents didn't trust her. But I thought they were
wrong about Kerry. I could see the good side of her, and
I wanted other people to see it too, and that's why I stayed
friends with her. But everything changed when Kerry went to
Queensland.

Kerry only did one day of Year 9 at my school. Things had
been getting more and more tense between her and her mum,
so after the first day of term she moved up to Queensland to
live with her auntie. But I guess that didn't work out either,

because one day early in June she called to tell me she was in Sydney again and living with her mum.

'I'm back!' she said. 'Let's do something!'

My friends have always been really important to me. If somebody needs me, I'm always there for them. There are people who won't lift a finger to help anyone, even if they're in serious trouble, even if they're practically dead, but that's not me. I'll do just about anything to help a friend. Kerry and me were really close before she went away, and I'd missed her. I really wanted to see her again. We arranged that I would sleep over at her house that Friday and Saturday night. Kerry's mum was working night shift, which meant the night was ours.

'What do you want to do?' I asked.

'I know some people who are having a party,' Kerry said. 'You want to go?'

I liked parties. Good music, interesting people, talking and dancing, fun. Why wouldn't I want to go?

'Whose party is it?' I asked. 'Do I know them?'

'No, but you'll like them. They're cool.'

'Sounds great,' I said. 'Let's go.'

'Okay.' Kerry paused. 'They said we could bring some friends if we wanted to. Do you know anyone else you could bring?'

'You mean like from school?'

'No, I mean somebody fun.'

I only had to think about it for a moment. 'I'll ask Sophie,' I said.

Sophie lived up the street from me. Although we went to different schools, we used to catch the same bus every day, and we got talking and became friends. Kerry had told me she wasn't coming back to our school – her mother was sending her to the local public school instead, which was where Sophie went. You know what high school's like – being there without any friends is the most depressing thing on earth, and if I introduced Kerry to Sophie, at least she'd know one other person at her new school. Besides, I had a feeling the two of them would probably hit it off.

Like Kerry, Sophie was a wild child. She was really fun to be around because she had no fear: if an idea came into her head she'd always say, 'Oh yeah, woo-hoo, let's go off and do this! Yeah!' I was always being told not to do anything wrong and not to do anything naughty, and if you're like me, if you get told often enough, eventually you just think, oh stuff it, I'm going to do the opposite. And whenever I was in the mood to do something naughty, I knew Sophie would always be up for it. We never did anything really bad though: we'd do things like waiting until all the teachers and students had gone home and then sneaking into the grounds of the primary school and hanging around on the play equipment. We never actually did any damage, we just liked the thrill of being somewhere we weren't supposed to be.

The thing about Sophie was, she didn't know when to stop. She got herself banned from Miranda, our local Westfield, for shoplifting. She had this thing about coloured pens –

highlighters and glitter pens – and she used to shoplift them and then get caught and they'd tell her she was banned from Miranda for two weeks, and she'd go right back in and steal more pens and get caught again and they'd ban her for even longer. It was a vicious cycle but you just couldn't stop her.

Sophie and Kerry were the two wildest girls I knew. My other friends all came from rich families and still thought a slumber party and glueing lollies on the head of the first girl who fell asleep was fun. I was pretty much over all that, and I was ready to go out and break a few rules. I was sure that putting my two wildest friends together pretty much guaranteed a good night. I don't know what I thought was going to happen that evening but I knew that there would be no parents, no bedtimes, no stupid pranks, no movie marathons and no rich kids, and that was good enough for me.

Now all I had to do was convince Nan to let me go.

'I TOLD YOU, NAN, it's a Nutrimetics party.'

Nan was grilling me for the *hundredth* time on what I was doing that night. I wasn't really too sure what we were doing, but Kerry's mum was a Nutrimetics salesperson and I thought a Nutrimetics party would be a good cover story for whatever we were really going to get up to.

'Look, all we're doing is trying on make-up and just hangin' out with old people.'

My nan looked at me with the most disbelieving look and said, 'What friends of yours are going?'

'Just Sophie and Kerry,' I said. 'You can speak to Kerry's mum if you like.'

She had nothing else to say – my story was flawless. Unbelievably unbelievable. But flawless. She'd asked me over and over again what I was doing and I didn't slip up once. But telling her she could call Kerry's mum was the masterstroke: Nan *hated* talking to parents and I knew she'd never ever talk to them. She won't confront people. So I knew there was no chance she'd call me on it.

'Okay,' she said.

I'd done it. I was free.

GRANDAD DROVE ME TO Kerry's and waited in the car out the front of her unit block until I went in. I waved goodbye and walked up the stairs. Kerry's mum opened the door and told me the girls had gone to Sophie's to get a few things. Great, I thought. I've been left alone with Kerry's mum.

Kerry's mum had always scared me a little bit. She was a bit of a loose cannon. She'd had a lot of things go wrong in her life – she got divorced from her husband, then he got sick with cancer, so she went back and nursed him until he died, and then she was a single mother to her three kids, who all had major problems – one kid was a drug addict and one of them was a stripper with a young son, and Kerry, who was the youngest, was well on the way to being in trouble too. Kerry's mum had to work nights to pay the rent, so she was always tired and cranky. She wasn't exactly the most warm 'n' fuzzy person on the planet. If you knew her set of problems you kind of understood where her negative outlook came from, but that didn't make it any easier to listen to. All she could talk about was how bad the world was and how screwed up her kids were, and no matter what she did there was nothing she could do to make things better so why try? She made you feel so bad about life, and I knew from experience there was no point trying to cheer her up or getting her to see the bright side of things. For her it was all black. So I just sat there and listened while she ranted.

Finally Kerry and Sophie came back and Kerry proceeded to fight with her mum while Sophie and I snuck off to Kerry's bedroom to get changed out of our school clothes and into what we were going to wear that night.

Sophie had brought a white top and denim jeans with pink stitching up the side, and when she put them on she looked fantastic. Sophie was very good-looking – she had blonde hair and a beautiful face, and the only thing that spoilt it was the fact that sometimes she could be a bit stinky. There were times when you just had to say 'Sophie, here, use some deodorant. Put it on!' But this wasn't one of those times.

I'd brought a denim skirt and a red halter-neck top. My clothes weren't as fashionable as hers, but then again, I was an extremely large child and it was hard to find fashionable clothes that fitted me. I was bursting at the seams in anything I put on . . . so, I had to deal with what I had.

'Did Kerry tell you any more about this party we're going to?' I asked.

Sophie shrugged. 'All I know is we're leaving at seven.'

Kerry walked into the room then and she started to smile a wicked smile.

'Check this out,' she said, and then she opened her drawer and pulled out some condoms.

I was probably the most naïve fourteen-year-old you would ever meet in your entire life, but I had no idea why she was showing us condoms. I knew what they were, but I didn't actually believe people our age had sex. I didn't think people had sex till they were older – like, eighteen older. I was pretty stupid.

'What d'you need those for?' I said to her.

'What do you think? I've been doing this for ages!'

I just looked at her. I couldn't believe she'd say something like that. She'd been doing *what* for ages? She'd been having sex for ages?! Kerry was my age. Kerry was younger than me by about a month. Most of the girls my age couldn't even talk about periods yet, let alone sex – it was too embarrassing. But Kerry didn't look embarrassed. She looked proud.

'I think my mum knows 'cos the last time I did it I had this happy glow about me. I think she could tell,' Kerry said, sounding kind of smug and experienced.

I didn't know whether to believe Kerry or not. She had been

known to spin a few good stories before and I wasn't sure if this was one of them . . . but she seemed to know what she was talking about, and that shocked me. Not just because she was having sex, but because she was so comfortable with the idea that her mum might know about it. I would *die* if my grandparents or my mum ever thought I was having sex! I didn't want *anybody* to know about all that stuff! It was too 'yuck' for me.

Kerry started getting changed to go out. Kerry was short – I was always paying her out about it – with light brown, frizzy hair and massive boobs. (I had no boobs at all.) She could look really pretty when she did herself up, but she seemed to prefer dressing like a homey in baggy men's clothes. That night she put on baggy pants and a men's basketball shirt.

'What are you wearing that for?' I teased her. 'That stuff is *so* unflattering! I thought we were going to a party.'

But Kerry just laughed, telling me to piss off.

We quickly ate dinner – home-made chunky soup and a little bit of spag bol – and got out of there fast. Kerry's mum was yelling at us as we walked out . . . I wasn't too sure what she was yelling and none of us really cared. We didn't have much respect for Kerry's mum, and after listening to her ranting for an hour, I was desperate to get away from her and let the fun begin.

We fooled around as we walked to Miranda station, talking about absolute pointless shit. I'm famous for being a bit of a motormouth, but Kerry and Sophie were leaving me for dead.

And the more I listened to Kerry the more I began to realise how much she'd changed while she was away in Queensland. She'd always been a bit wild, but now she was *really* wild.

Before Kerry left, the stuff she'd got up to had been harmless enough. She'd tried to get me to smoke cigarettes once, but that was about as bad as it got. Now, though, the stuff she was getting up to was really bad. She'd been kicked out of her auntie's for drinking and refusing to go to school. She was talking about gangs and drinking and about her sister being a stripper. She never used to think this was a good thing before – she used to be really ashamed of it, and I was one of the few people who knew what her sister did for a living. But now she was acting like she was proud of it. I don't know what happened to her in Queensland, but something had changed her. This was not the girl I'd known before.

We got on the train and Kerry and Sophie started talking about sex at the tops of their voices. I was so embarrassed that I got up and moved seats, but they just thought that was hysterical and started talking even louder. There were people listening to us and staring, but Kerry didn't care. The more she got stared at, the more outrageous she became, and Sophie went right along with her. Sophie didn't have a clue what she was talking about – she was just egging Kerry on. But it was clear already that these two had really hit it off. My match-making skills had been spot-on: Kerry and Sophie had clicked from the minute they met, and now they were busy working themselves up into a fever of excitement, and even though

I was embarrassed by them it was hard not to get swept up in it.

'So where are we going?' I asked finally, desperate to change the topic.

'We're going to Sutho,' Kerry said, meaning Sutherland station, 'and Mustapha's picking us up.'

'Picking us up?' I asked. 'Isn't he our age?'

'Yeah, but his brother's driving.'

For the first time, I began to feel that there was something not quite right about the evening. It was one thing if we were going to hang out with someone our own age, but if his older brother was going to be there too – a guy who was old enough to drive – that felt different. Don't ask me why, but it did. But it was nothing I could put my finger on, so I stayed quiet.

The train finally pulled up at Sutho and we walked across the road to a convenience store to wait for Mustapha and his brother. There was a guy there who Kerry knew – she said he was her cousin, although he wasn't. The two of them started having this long conversation that very obviously didn't include me or Sophie. So we stood around checking out the magazines and the chocolate bars while we waited for whatever was going to happen next.

Kerry had a lot of ethnic friends – especially ethnic guys – who she liked to call 'bro' or 'cousin'. Most of them were Lebanese, although I later discovered that the boys we were meeting that night were actually from Pakistan. It wasn't a common thing to have ethnic friends in our neighbourhood, the Shire, mainly because the majority of the people are surfers from Cronulla.

Sutherland Shire is in southern Sydney, near Cronulla Beach, and it was made famous by the Cronulla riots. The Shire isn't racist, but it is extremely white and Anglo – the people who live there don't have much contact with people from other cultures, so to go looking for friends from out-side was pretty unusual. But Kerry thought these guys were fantastic. She'd met them about a year earlier through a friend from the PCYC – the Police and Community Youth Club – and she'd gradually become more and more friendly with them. I had never really been involved in this side of Kerry's life – not because she didn't want me to, but because I never really liked the sound of it. I'd always thought she was mad for hanging out with some of these guys because they sounded so dodgy. They were always giving her things, like clothes and mobile phones, and they'd promised they would always protect her. What that meant was, they'd beat people up for her. I couldn't see why a fourteen-year-old schoolgirl needed protection, but Kerry loved it. Once before she left for Queensland she asked me if I wanted an eighteen-year-old boyfriend. I said hell no – for one thing, I didn't know any guy on the planet who wanted to go out with a baby hippo, but also I couldn't fathom the age difference. She never asked me about it again.

After we'd been waiting in the convenience store for a while we heard this loud bass music coming from up the road. We all looked around, and Kerry said, 'Yup . . . that's them. I always know when they're coming by the loud music.'

Kerry went rushing out of the convenience store to meet them, and so Sophie and I followed her.

A dark Skyline was parked on the other side of the road and it was practically shaking from the music. Two boys stepped out of the car as we crossed the road. Kerry gave them both a kiss on each cheek and then introduced us to them.

'Amir, this is Tegan and Sophie.'

Amir was a tall Lebanese-looking man, who I guessed was in his twenties, with shoulder-length hair that was tied at the back in a ponytail. I was a little shocked when I saw just how old he was; I didn't think this was such a good idea anymore. He leant over and gave both me and Sophie a kiss on each cheek. I thought this was a little weird. I was used to the usual, 'Yeah, I'll shake your hand . . .' or the no-contact hand-in-the-air kind of wave. I wasn't used to getting a kiss on each cheek. It just wasn't done in the Shire.

'And this is Mustapha.'

He was shorter than Amir and looked a little younger, maybe seventeen. He had all his hair shaved off except for his fringe. It was a fairly long fringe with about four inches of brown regrowth. The rest of it was peroxide blonde and it got thinner as it went to the back of his head. It was probably the most ugly-looking haircut I'd ever seen. Just as his brother had, Mustapha bent down and gave me a kiss on each cheek, then did the same with Sophie.

By now I was starting to feel uneasy. Now that I'd heard their names I knew they were Kerry's dodgy friends, and I didn't know if I was comfortable hanging out with them. I looked at Amir and wondered if he was the one Kerry had tried to get me to go out with. If he was, that was really creepy.

My instincts were telling me to get out of there. Something didn't feel right about these guys or this situation. But, I told myself, we were going to a party. If these guys turned out to be as dodgy as I suspected, I could always find someone else to talk to.

Kerry had the car door open and was ready to climb in.

'Are you guys coming or what?' she said.

Sophie looked at me and shrugged and climbed into the car with Kerry.

I could have followed my instincts and said no. I could have turned around and got back on the train and gone home again. But seriously, what fourteen-year-old is really going to do that? How could I tell Kerry that I had a bad feeling about these guys? She would have been totally insulted.

I climbed into the back seat of the car. Wherever we were going, I was in.

And besides, I was with my friend Kerry. She wouldn't let anything bad happen to me. Right?

# 3

# Stolen innocence

THE INSIDE OF THE car was lit a brilliant neon-blue by the stereo, and the music was so loud I thought I was going to have a heart attack. The car seats were vibrating from the sub-woofers in the back, making it hard for me to breathe. I kept quiet and focused on Amir's hair. His long ponytail was tied with a gross fluoro-green elastic hair tie. It looked like the kind of elastic they use on braces to align your jaw.

By now I was really starting to worry. We were in a car with two dodgy guys and I had no idea where we were going. I kept thinking, *What if something bad happens tonight? What if they do something stupid? What if they try to rape us? What if they try to bash us?* I had no reason to think anything was going to happen. But I couldn't stop worrying. Eventually I decided if anything bad happened I'd just grab Sophie and run. I thought Kerry could probably look after herself. I mean, she was my friend, and I didn't want to abandon her, but at the end of the day she'd brought us here, and she was a big girl. She could handle herself. But I felt responsible for Sophie.

At one point Kerry turned to me and asked, 'Why are you so quiet? Normally you never shut up.'

I wanted to tell her her mates were freaking me out, but I didn't want to say it in front of them – that would have been rude. 'I'm thinking, that's all,' I said, and fell silent again.

Then Mustapha turned the music down and started talking to us. The two guys had very heavy accents and every so often they would say something to each other in a foreign language, which I later found out was Pashtu. Kerry seemed to know what they were saying, 'cos she'd let out a little giggle, although I don't know how much she really understood. She would say the odd word to them and to me it sounded like she was agreeing with them. Maybe what they were saying was completely harmless, but it didn't exactly make me feel calmer, listening to them saying things I couldn't understand.

After a while the car stopped and the boys got out.

'We're just going to take a piss,' Mustapha explained. 'We had a few vodkas and we wanna get it out of our system just in case we get breathalysed.'

I didn't know if that'd actually work, but hey, if they wanted to try it, why not?

We waited in the car while the guys took a leak. Kerry turned to me and Sophie. 'What d'you think of them?' she asked.

Sophie looked at me, then at Kerry. 'They're okay, I guess.'

'What about you, Tegan?'

This would have been the moment for me to say *Actually I think they're creeps. Let's get the hell out of here.* But it was winter, we were miles from home, we had no money – and besides, I knew Kerry was really into them and if I insulted them it was going to cause major problems between us. So all I said was, 'I don't know. I don't really know them . . .'

The boys got back into the car then and took us to look for an ATM and a bottlo.

'What do you want?' Mustapha asked, when we found the bottle shop.

Kerry answered for us. 'Get whatever,' she said.

'Do you girls drink vodka? It makes your head less sore in the morning.'

'Yeah. Get some of that,' Kerry said. 'And Coke.'

This was getting worse and worse. They were buying us alcohol now?

'Where are we?' I asked. I didn't recognise this place at all.

'We're in Ashfield,' Kerry said. 'We're going back to their house.'

It occurred to me that she must have known all along that this was where we were going, but she hadn't told me. Maybe she knew that if she had, I wouldn't have agreed to come.

Sophie was looking out the back window. 'What's that writing for?' she asked.

'Oh, that's for Tahir's work. This is his work car,' Kerry said.

'Who's Tahir?' asked Sophie.

'He's Mustapha's older brother,' Kerry said dismissively. She turned to me. 'Tegan, have you ever gotten drunk before?'

I thought about it for a moment and then I said, 'No, I've never gotten drunk before.'

'That's because you've never drunk alcohol before.'

'No, I haven't,' I said. I'd drunk shandies before – not very strong ones mixed by my mum – but it didn't occur to me that that's what she meant.

She got all aggressive for no reason. 'Tell me the fucking truth right now! Have you ever gotten drunk?'

I was a bit taken aback. I didn't expect her to act like this. '*No*, Kerry, I haven't. I've never been drunk.'

Kerry turned to Sophie. 'What about you?'

'Yeah, I have a few times.'

'Okay, good,' Kerry said. 'Well you can both drink a mix then.'

I had no idea what a 'mix' was, but Kerry was being so weird and aggressive I didn't want to ask.

Then the boys came back and started driving again.

'So do youse girls take drugs?' Amir asked. 'We can get you some weed, do you want some weed?'

Now I was getting really worried. They were offering us drugs now?

24

'No,' I said. Sophie shook her head. Kerry just made an impatient sound, as if we were spoiling her night.

The boys pulled up yet again, this time at a shopping centre, so they could go in and buy some Coke, and while they were at the shop I decided it was time I let Kerry know I wasn't happy about the way our night was shaping up.

'I thought you said everyone was going to be *our* age, Kerry,' I said.

'Mustapha *is* our age,' Kerry said.

'Yeah, but what about Amir? He's not.'

It should have been obvious by now that I wasn't comfortable about any of this. But if Kerry realised, she didn't let it bother her. 'Who cares, Tegan?' she said. 'Just relax and have fun.'

The boys came back with the Coke. We drove off again and finally pulled up in this weird driveway. It went round in a bit of a bend and then stopped at a garage which was falling to pieces with bits of asbestos broken off it. The boys jumped out and moved the seat so we could jump out as well. I got tangled up climbing out and practically fell out the door, embarrassing myself and breaking the chain off my anklet.

'Are you sure you've never been drunk before, Tegan?' Kerry said, and laughed.

I was surprised when I saw their house. The car the boys drove was pretty upmarket, but the house was old and shabby-looking, with bars on the windows. They took us into the house through the back door. Kerry told us to take off our shoes and leave them at the door. 'It's a sign of respect,' she said.

We walked through into the lounge room and were greeted by three more boys. Kerry started introducing us to all of them.

'This is Sabir, Rashid and Boo – they're Mustapha's brothers.'

All of them gave us a kiss on each cheek. It creeped me out and I wished everyone would stop doing it. I do have a thing called personal space, but they didn't seem to know about that.

'Where's the party?' I asked Kerry.

'This is it,' she said.

The lounge had two couches in it, one of them bent like a banana, and there was a coffee table in the middle. The three of us sat down and the boys started pouring us drinks – vodka and Coke – and gave each of us a cigarette.

I had no idea how to smoke. Even though I'd tried it a couple of times I'd never quite got the hang of it. Kerry tried to show me how it was done.

'You're just bum-puffing it,' Kerry said. 'You've got to draw back.'

She sucked the smoke down into her lungs and then blew it out again, but whenever I tried I just coughed.

'Hey Kerry,' one of the boys said, 'put your phone on the table, okay?'

Kerry pulled her phone out of her bag and put it on the

coffee table, just like they asked. Neither me or Sophie had a mobile.

'And don't answer it if it rings, eh?' he added.

I was definitely feeling a little bit freaked out by all this: the long car trip, the cheek-kissing, the pile of shoes at the door, the weird house, the roomful of older guys, the drinks they were pushing on us. And now they were making Kerry give up her phone. I could sense trouble.

'So how old are you girls?' Sabir asked.

'Fifteen,' I said.

'Fifteen,' said Soph.

In fact we were both still fourteen, just – my birthday is on 28 July, and Soph's not long after, so we were still about six weeks short. But we were both close enough to fifteen that it didn't seem to matter. Kerry's birthday was later in the year.

'I'm fourteen,' she said.

'Why do you have to put your phone on the table?' I asked her.

'It's just rude to come all the way out here and then be on the phone to someone else,' she said.

I didn't believe her, but I took that as the answer anyway. With five strange guys in the room, what else was I going to do?

Then Mustapha sat down next to Sophie and started cracking onto her. He was trying to sweet-talk her, nibbling on her ear, putting his hands all over her. I could tell she didn't like it from the way she kept looking over at me, but she put up with it.

Rashid and the other boys kept pouring us more drinks and making us drink them by saying, 'Cheers!' and then telling us we had to drink because it would be rude not to.

It didn't occur to me that vodka and Coke was very different from beer mixed with lemonade. I didn't understand that different kinds of alcohol really do have different strengths. And of course I had no idea how much vodka was in those drinks either. So I kept knocking them back. And the guys kept pouring more.

It didn't take long before I started feeling light-headed and tipsy. It wasn't a bad feeling – just a strange one. I'd never been tipsy before so this was all new to me. I started dropping in and out of other people's conversations, trying to learn what I could about these people we'd ended up with, and for a while I felt things were going okay. But then I heard Rashid offering to get Kerry a gun.

'Yeah, a pistol with one shot,' he said. 'So you can protect yourself.'

That was scary – not just because they were talking about guns, but because they were offering to get my friend one. What would Kerry do with a gun? And why would she even need one? I made a mental note to myself: *I have to talk to Kerry about that later – I can't let her think that's a good idea.*

Rashid was explaining that he and his brothers carried knives. 'You never know when you're going to have to defend yourself,' he said. 'If you keep it in the sleeve of your jacket it's easy to get at and no one knows you've got it.' They then proceeded to tell me that they had used these knives on someone who was picking on their brother at school. The knives had come out *after* the little brother had thrown a garbage bin at a teacher.

I was now officially freaked out.

Kerry got up then and went out of the room with Mustapha, and Sophie started nudging me with her toes, mouthing the words, 'Help me.' It was pretty clear that she didn't like Mustapha cracking onto her and she wasn't going to put up with it any longer.

When Kerry came back into the room I pulled her aside. 'I'm pretty sure Sophie hates Mustapha,' I whispered. 'She wants him to piss off.'

Kerry sat down next to Sophie and whispered in her ear, and I assumed she was saying something like, 'Don't worry, I'll get you out of here.' But then Mustapha sat down and started nibbling Sophie's other ear, which was quite a grotesque sight, and Kerry started talking about what a great guy Mustapha was.

'Why are you being so uptight, Sophie?' Kerry said. 'Mustapha's a really great guy. I know heaps of girls who'd die to be where you are right now.'

Mustapha was smirking into her ear. Sophie was just giving me a 'get me out of here' stare so I decided it was time to help her out.

'I don't think her boyfriend'd be too happy about that,' I said.

The boys turned and looked at me. They weren't happy. 'Have you got a boyfriend?' Mustapha asked.

'Yeah,' Sophie said, although she didn't.

The brothers all looked at each other then and Mustapha said something to Kerry. She just shrugged and looked annoyed, as if she was saying *it isn't my fault*. But after that, the boys left Sophie alone.

Someone put another drink in my hand. I didn't know how many drinks I'd had by this stage but I swear, they were getting stronger.

I decided it was time to go to the bathroom. It wasn't until I stood up that I discovered just how drunk I really was. I was stumbling all over the place. I could barely walk. I fell a few times into the wall. It took all my powers of concentration to get myself to the bathroom and not do anything stupid.

When I finally made it to the bathroom I cracked up when I saw myself in the mirror, because I knew I was drunk and I thought I looked so funny. I stood there laughing for a while and then I went back into the lounge room, feeling my way along the walls.

When I got back Kerry was still trying to convince Sophie that Mustapha was a fantastic guy. 'I bet you'd really be into him if you gave him a chance,' Kerry was saying. All I could think was, *Give it up already – she doesn't like him!* It didn't occur to me that there might be a reason why she was so keen for Sophie to hit it off with Mustapha – that that might be why

Kerry had been asked to bring another girl along. I thought we were just there to hang out and chat.

And drink.

There was no more room for me to sit on the banana couch with Kerry and Sophie, so I sat on the other one, next to one of the other guys, whose name I'd forgotten. He looked the oldest. His hair was short and he smelt of BO. He put his arm around me and started talking to me. This was more physical contact I didn't feel comfortable with, and the way he smelt made me feel a bit sick. But I told myself to be cool about it – it was the kind of thing your brother would do, and it wouldn't bother me if it was my brother, so why should it bother me now? And as for all that talk about knives and guns, I told myself they were Kerry's friends; she had always said these guys would protect her, so why would they hurt us?

A song came on – Shakira's 'Whenever, Wherever' – and I started singing along, trying to pretend that none of this was happening. Then Amir came and sat on the other side of me and put his hand on my inner thigh. I didn't like this at all. I wasn't used to this sort of attention and I didn't have the faintest idea how to handle it. I was so self-conscious about my body that I never thought a guy would think of me as pretty or look at me in a sexual way. I thought that guys just thought I was one of the boys – someone fun to hang around with. So when Amir put his hand on my thigh I didn't know what to do. I remembered what I'd decided back in the car – *if anything bad happens, I'll grab Sophie and run*.

I didn't run, because as long as the three of us were together I didn't believe anything too bad could happen. But every time Kerry got up and left the room, leaving me and Sophie with all those guys, it started to feel really creepy – especially once those two guys started leaning all over me. I knew I needed to get up off that couch and away from those two guys and onto the other couch where Kerry and Sophie were sitting, but I was too shy to say, 'Hey, get the hell off me!' So instead I tried to think of a polite way to get away, and I decided I'd say I was going to the bathroom. That would work. And when I came back I'd sit with the girls and it would all be okay.

I got up and discovered I could barely stand. I walked through the doorway, holding onto the door as I headed towards the bathroom. When I got to the bathroom I locked the door and sat there for a minute, trying to clear my head. I knew I needed a plan – what was I going to do next? How would I avoid getting trapped again? I drank some water out of the tap and went to the toilet. I waited a little bit longer and I thought, *All right, you have to go back out there; but when you go back out there sit on the couch and don't look at anybody.*

I stood up and opened the bathroom door. I had to hold onto the wall as I tried to walk back to the lounge room. To this day, I've never been so drunk. I got to the lounge room door, and then one of the guys grabbed my hand and said, 'I need to talk to you.'

He pulled me through another door into a room I hadn't been into before. The lights were switched off and the room was dark, although there was a little light shining through the curtains from the streetlights outside. I got an impression of bars on the window. A lot of what happened next is a blur.

At first I couldn't tell who had grabbed me, but then I caught a glimpse of his ponytail and realised it must be Amir. He was babbling to me about something but I didn't understand anything he was saying. I couldn't take anything in. I was way too drunk. The next thing I remember was him trying to kiss me. I tried to push him away, telling him, 'I don't want to do this!' I was so disorientated, I had no idea where I was. All I knew was I was sitting on a bed with a boy I didn't know, who was trying to kiss me. I didn't want him to – I knew that much. I got up and tried to leave and rejoin my friends, but he wouldn't let me leave the room. He pushed me back down onto the bed and started talking to me. I think he was trying to calm me down.

'Have you got a mobile phone? I can get one for you. Do you want a phone?'

I couldn't focus on anything. I could barely move. I was too drunk.

'What do you think of marriage? Are you going to get married one day or don't you believe in it?'

*Marriage?* I wanted to say. *How should I know? I'm fourteen!* The whole conversation was just bizarre.

I tried to get up again and he pushed me back down onto

the bed. I couldn't move anymore. I felt like I had bricks tied to my arms and legs and they were weighing me down. I knew I was in trouble.

'Please, I don't want to do anything,' I told him. 'I just want a coffee. Please can you get me a coffee? I need to be sober.'

But Amir ignored me and kept right on talking while he started touching my body. I kept zoning in and out; at first I wouldn't feel anything, but then all of a sudden I'd regain just a slight sensation in a part of my body and realise he was touching me. He couldn't keep his hands off me. But I was so drunk I couldn't push him away.

The next thing I remember was zoning out and coming to again when his hand was up my skirt. I tried to push his hand away and tell him not to do it but I couldn't muster the strength to push him away. I told him *not to* and he just said, 'Shhh . . .' and changed the subject. I kept trying to tell him not to, that I didn't want to be doing this, and every single time he'd hush me.

He put his hand up underneath my top and started feeling what little breasts I had. I was only fourteen. I was very undeveloped. I didn't have breasts. I still don't have breasts. I'm barely an A-cup. I never ever thought that it'd be something a guy would want to feel – there's nothing there. Yet he did. He put his hand up underneath my top and started feeling my breasts. I didn't know what to do. His hands were going all over my body and I couldn't stop him. I kept trying to muster up the strength to get up and every time I did, he'd push me back down.

Rays of light kept coming through the door. I think his mates were trying to say something to him, but they were speaking in Pashtu so I couldn't understand anything they were saying. I tried to get the words together to say, 'Help me,' but I couldn't even do that. I couldn't get my voice to work.

I felt him remove my undies. He slid them down my legs and took them off. I wanted to grab them and pull them back up but I had no control over my body. I told him I didn't want to do this and he just hushed me again. I zoned out. The next thing I remember was him fingering me. I knew I didn't want him to be doing this but I couldn't push him off me, I couldn't push him away from me. He was taking control of my body and I couldn't even defend myself. I said to him, 'No, I don't want to be doing this!' and he just hushed me again.

Then Amir pushed my skirt up around my waist. I tried to pull it back down again but he was too strong. He lifted up my legs and there was nothing I could do to stop him. I felt like I was paralysed. My legs were like jelly. Heavy jelly. I could feel them, but I couldn't move them. I could feel everything around me, but I couldn't move. I zoned out again.

The next thing I remember was Amir thrusting backwards and forwards on top of me. He was raping me. I could feel him going in and out. I didn't want to look up because when I looked up I could see his face. I could see the outline of him and his ponytail. I wanted to cry but I didn't want him to see me cry. I wanted him to get off me and fuck off! All I wanted was for it to stop. I didn't want to be there anymore. I wanted him to get away from me and as soon as he got away from me I wanted to jump into a big bath of disinfectant. I just wanted to be home and safe in bed.

Every so often I'd see the door open again. He'd yell something at the door and they'd yell something back. The door would close. I couldn't hear my friends anymore.

One more time I said, 'No, I don't want to do this. I'm only fourteen. Get off me!'

He didn't try and hush me this time. He didn't say anything at all, he just kept going. I could feel him, going in and out. I put my hands over my face and tried to think about something else. I tried to think about another place. Finally I just tuned out. It was the only defence I had. I couldn't move. I couldn't kick him off me. Saying 'no' didn't seem to be enough. The only defence was for me to tune out and not be there anymore. Just leave my body. So that's what I did.

Finally, he stopped. He got up, fixed himself up, and walked out of the room. I sat up and tried to find my underpants and put them back on. Then another guy came into the room and pushed me back down onto the bed. I couldn't muster the energy to sit back up again. I was so drunk, I couldn't do anything. When I looked at the guy who'd just walked in I couldn't see the outline of a ponytail anymore, so I knew it wasn't Amir.

'You're not the same guy as before,' I said. 'Who are you?'

But he didn't answer me. He sat down on the bed and started massaging my forehead.

'Please, can you leave me alone?' I said. 'I just want to be alone!'

But he wouldn't leave.

First, I thought since he was only massaging my forehead I should just put up with it until I could think of a way out of there. But then I decided no, I wasn't going to put up with it, and I tried to move my arm to push his hand away. But I was still so drunk I couldn't move properly, and he grabbed my arm and laid it down above my head. He started putting his penis and his balls onto my head. He tried to get me to play with them but I didn't want to touch him. I zoned out. I think I might've even fainted.

I really don't remember a lot of what happened after that. The next thing I do remember was him on top of me, raping me, just like his brother did.

'I don't want to do this!' I said. 'Get off me! Leave me alone!'

It hadn't worked with Amir and it didn't work with him either. He wouldn't stop.

The door started opening and closing again. I could hear voices speaking in another language. He answered them and they shut the door and then he kept raping me.

I tried hard to move, focusing all of my energy on just being able to lift up one part of my body so I could *hit* him, but

I couldn't even do that much. At last he stopped raping me, got up, and left the room.

I was alone at last. I felt so violated. Two guys had just raped me and I didn't even know who the second guy was. I didn't recognise him, I didn't recognise his voice. (It wasn't until we had the DNA samples tested that we discovered it was Sabir who'd raped me.) All I knew was that he didn't understand me when I was trying to tell him to get off me – or else he didn't care. It was like my feelings didn't matter, they just wanted their way. They'd gotten me drunk so they could rape me. I didn't want to be there! I didn't want this! I didn't want those boys to touch me! But they had.

I'd sobered up a bit by now, and I managed to find my underpants and put them back on. All I could think about was getting out of that room and out of that house.

I started for the door – and then another guy walked in.

'Hey, where are you going?' he said.

I recognised his voice. It was Mustapha – the one who had been trying to crack onto Sophie. I stood up and tried to leave. Mustapha put his hands on my arms to try to stop me, then put his head forward and started smothering me with his lips as he tried to kiss me. I pushed him away.

'I just had two guys rape me,' I told him. 'Please, let me go. I don't want to be here. I don't want to touch you and even if I did, I'd use a condom. I don't want to be here!'

'I've *got* a condom,' he said, completely ignoring everything else I'd said to him.

'I don't care!' I shouted. 'I don't want to be here, please. I just want to leave. Let me go!'

But he wouldn't let me go.

So I tried a new tactic. 'If you let me go to the bathroom, I'll come back,' I said. 'I really need to go to the toilet. I'm busting to go.'

He looked like he only half-believed me. 'You'll come back?'

'Yeah, I promise. As soon as I go to the bathroom, I'll come straight back.'

Of course I was really thinking, *As soon as I go to the bathroom, I'm going to bolt out that back door. I'm going to run to the nearest police station and then I'm going to tell them all what you guys have done!*

'Okay,' Mustapha said. 'You can go to the bathroom but you've got to promise to come straight back!'

'I promise!' I said.

I headed for the door, and for the second time that night I tripped over something – I think it was a small heater – and landed on a couch. I tried to get back up again and Mustapha was standing over me. He leant forward and I kicked him as hard as I could. He fell down and landed against the door, but before I could get up and get out of there he was on his feet, blocking the doorway. He slapped me across the face.

'Why you do this to me? Why you do this to me?' he kept saying, as if he was the one who'd been violated and not me.

He slapped me across the face again.

'Why did you do that to me?'

He hit me again.

'Do you want to get stabbed? Do you want me to take a knife and stab you?'

'No, I don't want you to stab me,' I said.

'So why you do this to me?'

'I don't want you to rape me. I don't want you to touch me.'

'Do you want me to stab you?'

I didn't want him to stab me . . . so I had to let him do it. He pushed me back down and started raping me.

He hurt a lot more than the others. For the first time that night I started to cry. 'Why are you doing this to me? Why me? Why are you doing this to me?'

'Because I'm fucking horny!' he snarled.

I just put my hands over my face and cried. I was being raped . . . again. And again, I couldn't do anything about it.

At last he stopped. He got up and turned the light on, pulling his pants up. There was a condom wrapper and a red condom on the floor. I looked at Mustapha with his awful peroxide haircut with the four inches of brown regrowth. He looked right back at me as if he didn't care if I could identify him. And then he walked out of the room as if nothing had happened.

I grabbed my underpants, put them back on, and then bolted out the door and ran to the bathroom before anyone else could grab me. I sat in the bathroom and bawled my eyes out. I couldn't quite believe what had just happened to me:

three men had raped me and my friends had done nothing to help me.

And I was still stuck in that house with no way out.

Someone tapped at the bathroom door and I froze. Were the rest of them going to come after me now? Was I going to have to climb out the bathroom window?

But then I heard Kerry say, 'Tegan, are you okay? Tegan, come out. What's wrong?'

I opened the door and Kerry and Sophie were both standing there. They must have known something was wrong, because they both hugged me.

'It's okay,' Kerry said. 'We're going.'

We were leaving. It was over.

# 4

# Traitors

THE FIRST THING I felt was relief – at last I was with my friends, they were going to help me, it was all going to be okay. They would get me out of here and I'd tell them what had happened and we'd go to the police and then the cops'd come here and arrest all of these guys.

But then Kerry said, 'They're going to drop us at the station,' and I realised she expected me to get back into a car with those guys.

'I'm not getting back in their car!' I said. 'They raped me!'

Kerry glanced over her shoulder. She was worried that the boys might have heard me. 'Just shut up and get in the car, Tegan,' she said.

We stopped to put our shoes on, and I discovered someone had taken mine from the back door where I'd left them. At the time I didn't think anything of it, but in hindsight I wonder whether they thought confiscating my shoes was another way of keeping me there. If they believed that, they don't know much about Australian women. I'm from the Shire, it's a very beachy culture, I never wear shoes. I would've run out of that house without my shoes. If I'd thought I could get away I would've run out of that house without my *clothes*! Leaving my shoes behind wouldn't have stopped me for one second. Knowing me, they probably cost me five bucks at Payless. I could've just bought another pair. If I'd got past Mustapha, I would have been out of there like a shot.

We got into the car and the boys drove us away. I sat there between my two friends, crying my eyes out. I kept trying to tell them what had happened, saying: 'They raped me, they raped me! Please, won't you listen to me? They raped me!'

But nobody wanted to listen to me. Kerry kept telling me to be quiet, while the boys got angrier and angrier.

'Shut up, bitch! Shut your friend up!'

But I was way past letting them talk like that to me. 'Fuck you!' I shouted. 'You raped me, you arseholes!'

But I could've been talking to a brick wall. Nobody said they were sorry, nobody asked if I was okay, nobody offered to help. Not Kerry. Not Sophie.

Finally, the car stopped outside the station. The three of us got out and I started to run. I thought if I got to the platform there'd be someone there who could help me. My friends had been useless but maybe there'd be someone at the station who'd know what to do.

I could hear one of the boys yelling: 'If you guys go to the police, we'll kill you!'

I ran to the platform and sat down and bawled my eyes out. The station was deserted. There was no one I could ask for help. For a while, no one followed me – not the boys, not my friends. Eventually Sophie came up the stairs, sat down next to me and put her arm around me.

'Where's Kerry?' I asked.

'She's still down there talking to them,' Sophie said. 'Are you okay?'

I shook my head and cried.

Eventually Kerry came up the stairs and joined us.

'I talked to them,' she said. 'It's all going to be okay, but you can't go to the cops.'

'But they raped me!'

'I don't think they would have done that, Tegan,' Kerry said.

'What are you talking about?' I yelled. 'I'm telling you they did!'

Kerry looked uncomfortable. 'You've got to see it from their point of view,' she said. 'They've been going through a really difficult time. Their friend was murdered. They were just taking out their anger on you, that's all.'

That was the moment it began to dawn on me that Kerry,

this girl I'd known and been friends with for two and a half years, was not my friend. I'd told her I was raped by three guys, and instead of offering to help, she was making excuses for them. I could see from the look on her face that the way she saw it, *I* was the problem, not the boys. I wanted to slap her across the face.

'It's over now,' Sophie said, trying to smooth things over. 'Let's just go home, okay? You're going to be all right.'

Our train came and the three of us got on. I spotted a guy sitting in our carriage wearing a security guard's uniform, and I thought maybe he'd know how to help me. I screamed as loudly as I could, 'I was raped! These boys raped me! Kerry's friends raped me!'

I was still crying my eyes out. Kerry was furious with me. 'Will you shut the fuck up?' she said.

But I could see I'd got the security guard's attention. 'Help me!' I screamed.

But Kerry wasn't going to let anyone else get involved. 'She's off her face on drugs,' she said. 'She's just hallucinating, nothing happened. Don't worry about her.'

I could see I'd lost him. The guard just thought we were a bunch of stupid girls being idiots. I was drunk all right, but I wasn't on drugs, I wasn't hallucinating, and something really had happened to me. I had been raped.

'Let's get her upstairs,' Kerry said to Sophie.

Sophie could have taken my side. She could have told the guy I was telling the truth and asked him to help us. But instead, she sided with Kerry. She took me by the arm and said, 'Come on, Tegan, don't make a scene. We're going upstairs now; just calm down, okay?'

The two of them pushed me down the aisle and up the steps to the top half of the train carriage, away from the security guard.

Sophie and Kerry had decided to gang up on me. They weren't going to help me, and they weren't going to let anyone else help me either.

I was alone.

I was still crying when we got off at Central station. Normally I'm not the kind of girl who cries but that night I just couldn't stop. I was an absolute mess – I was shaking, I felt sick, I was drunk, I barely knew where I was. I kept hoping someone would ask me what was wrong and try to help me. But no one did.

At last we got to Miranda station. I'd cried all the way from Ashfield to Miranda.

We walked past Miranda Fair and crossed the road at a set of lights. I'd been feeling sicker and sicker, and finally it all got too much for me. I stopped dead and threw up in the middle of the road. There were cars waiting for me to get off the crossing. But I was past caring.

The three of us turned into the road Kerry lived on, and started heading for her house.

'I want to go to the police,' I told Kerry. I wanted to walk into the police station and tell them everything that had happened. I wanted them to see me crying and know that I was telling the truth. But Kerry pulled me away.

'You can't go to the cops,' she said. 'I'm in a gang, all right? If they find out you've gone to the cops they'll kill me. They'll kill all of us!'

I tried to argue with her. 'What if I'm pregnant?' I said. 'I don't know if they used condoms or not – I could be pregnant. I need to do something about this!'

'Look, I'm not going to let a friend of mine get pregnant,' Kerry said. (As if it was something she could control.) 'If you *are* pregnant, you'll just have to have an abortion. The boys'll pay for it. They'll have to.'

I suppose in her mind, that would be the honourable thing for them to do.

Kerry's mum wasn't home when we got back to her unit. She was working the night shift and wouldn't be back until the morning.

'Kerry, please can I use your phone?' I asked. 'I need to call my cousin and talk to her. *Please*, can you let me do that?'

My cousin Sally lived in Ballina and she was my idol. I wanted to be just like her. She was the cool older girl who got a tattoo and looked gorgeous in everything she wore and had boyfriends. She got a tongue piercing so I wanted a tongue piercing. She got a tattoo so I wanted a tattoo. She was about four years older than me, which meant she was young enough to understand how I was feeling, but old enough to have some clue about what I should do next.

'Mum put a block on the phone 'cos I ran up a big phone bill,' Kerry said. She paused, looking at me, then said, 'But if you really want to call someone, you can call the Kids Help Line. It's free, so you should be able to call them from here.'

So I rang the Kids Help Line and told my story, and when I'd finished, the lady on the other end said, 'You sound very calm for someone who's just been raped.'

When bad things happen to me, once the worst is over I've always been able to calm down and think logically and process my thoughts thoroughly – and that's what I'd started doing. But the lady on the phone gave me the impression she didn't believe a word I was saying.

'If you're thinking of going to the police then you shouldn't have a shower,' she told me, 'because you'll need whatever evidence is left on your body.'

I didn't know what that meant but I just said, 'Okay.'

'You'll probably go into shock, so if you want to go to the police, now would be the time to do it.'

'My friend won't let me go to the police,' I said.

'It's your decision,' the lady said, sounding a bit irritated with me. 'You can do whatever you want.'

But after everything I'd been through, I didn't have the strength to get up and walk out of Kerry's house and go to the cops on my own. It was late, I was exhausted, I was sick, sore, and traumatised.

And besides, I was starting to doubt myself. What if I was wrong and Kerry was right? What if what had happened to me wasn't really rape? The lady at Kids Help Line hadn't sounded too sure. And the more I thought about it, the more I started to convince myself that it must have been all my fault. After all, I was drunk, and I'd kind of let the first one kiss me, and maybe if I'd really really tried I could have fought them off . . . The only reason I thought it might be rape was because the last guy, Mustapha, had slapped me across the face a few times and pushed me on the couch. If it wasn't for that one incident, I would've had myself convinced that it wasn't rape at all. I was fourteen and a virgin, I had no sexual experience, and I didn't even have a very clear idea about what rape was. And that night, all I could think about was how it must have been all my fault.

So I decided I'd just go to bed.

Just before we crashed for the night, Kerry said, 'Hey, if you really want to go to the police you should take your undies off and wrap them up in tissue paper so you'll know which ones they were in the morning.'

This seemed like good advice, so I wrapped my underpants up and put them safely away in my bag. It didn't occur to me to wonder why Kerry was finally doing something to help me when she'd been so insistent I shouldn't go to the police.

The other girls passed out pretty much straight away, but I couldn't sleep. I was lying on the floor in Kerry's room with just a few blankets as a mattress and another blanket on top of me. I had the heater on next to me but I was freezing cold. It was the middle of winter and I couldn't stop shivering. I decided the only way to get warm was to have a shower. I remembered what the Kids Help Line counsellor had said, so I didn't wash, I just let the hot water run over me, and by the time I got out of the shower I felt much better. I figured that I had my undies stashed safely in my bag, so that was all the evidence I was going to need anyway.

I went back to Kerry's room and lay down again. I tried to sleep but it just didn't happen for me. After a while I heard Kerry's mum come home. She opened the door to check on us – I pretended to be asleep – and then she went to bed herself.

I realised if she was home it must be early in the morning and I could probably go to Miranda Fair and call someone. So I took my wallet, told the girls I was going, and took off.

When I got there the doors were open, although the shops were all still shut. I walked in, found a pay phone and called my cousin Sally in Ballina. My auntie Sylvia answered the phone.

'Is Sally there?' I asked.

'She's at work,' my auntie said. 'She won't be home until this evening.'

'Oh,' I said, and a huge wave of disappointment washed over me. I'd really been counting on being able to speak to Sally. Now I didn't know what to do.

'Tegan, what's wrong?' she said. 'You sound like something's wrong. Are you okay?'

I liked Auntie Sylvie, she was young and hip, and I thought

maybe if I told her she'd understand. I started to cry again as I told her what had happened to me, and she cried too.

'Tegan,' she said, 'you can't let them get away with this. You have to go to the police. Okay?'

She was the first person I'd spoken to who sounded like she really believed me. 'Okay,' I said.

'I've got to go to work,' she said, 'but as soon as I'm finished I'll call your nan and tell her what happened.'

I didn't really want my nan to know, but I said, 'Okay.'

'Take care of yourself, okay?'

'I will.'

I hung up the phone and walked back to Kerry's. I was supposed to be staying at her house again that night; there was no way I was spending another night with her after what had happened, but I was too confused to know what else to do.

Up in Ballina, Auntie Sylvie got in her car and went to work, but as soon as she walked in the door she realised she couldn't wait until that evening to do something about it. She went straight home again and called my nan, and as soon as my nan got off the phone from Auntie Sylvie she called me at Kerry's.

'What's this I hear about you getting raped?' Nan said.

I hadn't expected to hear from her until the evening, so I wasn't ready to deal with this, especially since she sounded really angry. (Looking back, I don't think she was angry. I think she just didn't know how to handle the situation, but it sounded like anger to me.)

I told Nan what had happened, and as soon as I'd finished

she said, 'We're going to come pick you up. We'll meet you out the front.'

Kerry and Sophie were stirring by then. I told them my nan was coming to get me and I'd told her what had happened.

'You should have been here before,' Kerry said. 'The boys called. They said to say they're sorry about what happened.'

'Are you serious?'

I didn't believe for a minute that the boys had called, or that they were sorry. Kerry was just saying that so I wouldn't make trouble.

'They were just blowing off steam. They're really good people once you get to know them.'

'I'm going,' I said, and started getting my stuff together.

'Hey, have you got any money left?' Kerry asked.

'Why?'

'I need some for the train.'

I had a little bit of money left. Stupidly, I gave it to her. 'Where are you going?' I asked.

'Just to see some friends,' she said evasively.

I stared at her, wondering if the friends she was going to see were the boys who'd raped me.

I went outside to wait for my grandparents and Kerry and Sophie drifted out after me.

Both my grandparents pulled up in their car. 'We're taking Tegan to the police station,' my nan said. 'Are you girls coming with us?'

I knew what Kerry's answer would be: no. I turned to look

at Sophie, but she just looked uncomfortable. 'I'm going to hang with Kerry,' she said.

'Don't go to the cops, Tegan,' Kerry warned.

'I have to,' I said. 'I'm not going to let them get away with this.'

'Just remember, I warned you,' Kerry said.

And then Kerry and Sophie turned and ran up to Miranda train station.

# 5

# Morning after

THIS IS WHAT HAPPENS when you report a rape to the police.

Nan and I walked into our local police station, and Nan walked up to the counter.

'I want to report a rape,' she said.

The policeman behind the counter gave us a bit of a funny look, but he went away and came back with two detectives, Kellie Salter and Kevin Bale. The detectives took me into an interview room and asked if they could have all the clothes I'd been wearing that night. I handed them over – and that was when I discovered that my underwear was missing.

'I can't find my undies,' I said. 'Last night I wrapped them up in tissues and put them in my bag so they wouldn't get lost, but now I can't find them.'

'Are you sure you put them in your bag?'

'I'm positive,' I said. 'It was Kerry's idea. She told me to wrap them up.' That was when the horrible realisation struck me. 'She must have taken them and hidden them somewhere.'

'Why would she do that?'

'To protect the guys who did this.'

When she'd suggested to me I should put my undies somewhere safe I'd thought she was finally being a friend to me. But it was becoming clearer by the second, Kerry was no friend of mine. Not anymore.

(Much later, I discovered that the police got a warrant to search Kerry's house, and they found my undies in a rubbish bin. Kerry had taken them out of my bag and thrown them away so there wouldn't be any evidence of what had happened to me that night. She should have tried a bit harder, because my underwear became a valuable source of evidence when we went to trial.)

Answering questions about what happened when you've just been raped was never going to be easy. But just to make things harder, my nan was there in the room, along with my grand-father and Nan's twin sister, my auntie Geraldine. I wasn't getting on well with my grandfather – our personalities clashed and we were always getting into fights about everything – and my family were shocked and upset and traumatised by what had happened, but to me it just looked like anger. I was still worried about getting into trouble for sneaking out with Kerry, so the last thing I wanted to do was go into all the gory details in front of my grandparents.

'Guys,' I said, 'you don't have to stay if you don't want to.'

'Of course I want to be here,' Nan said. 'We're not leaving you to do this alone.'

I would have much preferred to do it alone, but they were not getting the message. I tried appealing to my auntie Geraldine.

'Auntie Geraldine, don't you think it'd be better if you guys waited outside for a bit?'

That set my nan off – she started to yell.

I think the detectives could see we weren't going to get far if everybody was screaming and yelling, so they took me off to another room where they could question me in private.

Once I was alone with Kellie and Kevin they asked me to tell my story. I told them what had happened, and they listened and took notes, and then they started asking me questions. At first I felt sure they didn't believe me. They asked questions like: 'Were you a virgin before this? Are you sure you were a virgin before this? Are you sure it was actual rape?' It was like an interrogation, like I was the one who'd done something wrong. They questioned me for about an hour, and some of the things they asked me seemed like sensible questions: they asked if I knew the boys, where I knew them from.

They wanted to know how much alcohol I'd drunk. But they also wanted to know other things, like whether I used tampons, which didn't seem relevant at all.

The whole process was pretty intimidating. I was still in shock, and I was completely exhausted, and the way they were questioning me made me doubt myself even more than I already had been. I really needed someone to reassure me that what I'd experienced *was* rape, because in spite of everything I still wasn't completely sure. It's like when you're getting ready to go out somewhere and you call up your friend and say, 'Hey do you like this top? Should I wear this?' You need your friend to say, 'Yeah, wear that, you look good, you're okay.' And when someone doesn't say it, you start to think, 'Oh okay . . . I look like an idiot.' And this was the same. I needed someone to say to me, 'Yes, Tegan, you were raped, and you've done the right thing by coming here and talking to us.' But no one said it.

Eventually they must have decided they did believe me, because they told me they were going to take me to the hospital to get me checked out. We dropped Kevin off at Cronulla police station so he could get ready to take my statement once I was finished at the hospital. Kellie took me to the hospital. She was going to be there for the whole process.

I was sorry when we dropped Kevin off. Kellie was a pretty cool, detached sort of person (although I was grateful to her for rescuing me from my grandparents) but Kevin was relaxed, friendly, and funny.

'Where did you get Mustapha when you kicked him?' he asked as we were driving over to Cronulla.

'I think I might've kicked him in the balls,' I replied.

We had a bit of a chuckle about that. It made me feel a lot better because it finally felt like somebody was on my side.

THE HOSPITAL WAS AN ordeal.

First of all, I was taken for an examination. They looked for injuries and took swabs from inside me so they could test for semen or DNA. They asked the same questions the police had asked: Did I use tampons? (Yes.) Had I been a virgin? (Yes.) They asked questions about my menstrual cycle too, although I had no idea why that was relevant. And as if that wasn't embarrassing enough, they filmed the whole examination. The video camera was attached to a monitor, so I could see exactly what they were seeing – and that was pretty confronting. There they were, my genitals, larger than life on a monitor. I'd never seen them up close and personal before, and my first reaction was surprise: *Right, so that's what I look like from that angle* . . . But there's something really horrible about being exposed like that in front of a whole room full of people – the doctor, another woman who was supervising, my nan and grandfather, Kellie, a counsellor . . . Kellie was starting to make me nervous, because I still wasn't sure if she believed me; I was starting to feel pretty hysterical from the stress and the lack of sleep, and I began to worry that she was getting

59

ready to arrest me for something. The way she moved around the room made me think she was positioning herself to cut off my escape. So that made a humiliating situation worse.

After that, the needles started.

I hate needles – I've been terrified of them since I was a little girl. The sight of them makes me freak out. Sometimes I'll actually pass out. And that day at the hospital they treated me like a pincushion. They had to take a lot of blood, and then they had to blast me full of a whole lot of different medications. I couldn't handle it and threatened to pass out, which scared the living daylights out of my nan. A nurse had to put a numbing patch on my arm so I could make it through all the blood tests and injections.

They gave me an injection for HIV, an injection for two different types of hepatitis, and an injection for chlamydia. They took blood to test my cholesterol, and more blood to test for STDs. They told me that you couldn't detect some STDs until three months after you've been exposed to them, so I had to be tested now to prove that I didn't have any diseases before the rapes, then I'd have to go back for more blood tests in three months' time and more in six months' time to make sure I wasn't infected. It was a lot to take in: 24 hours ago I was a virgin. Now, there was a possibility I might have hepatitis or HIV, and it would be six months before I could be sure I was in the clear.

There was also a possibility I was pregnant, so one of the other things they gave me was the morning-after pill.

'What is this?' I asked.

'It'll stop you getting pregnant,' they said.

So I took it, just like I'd taken all the other things they'd given me that day. But as soon as I put it in my mouth I started to have doubts about whether it was the right thing to do.

I'm Catholic and I come from a Catholic family. We don't believe in abortion. By taking this pill was I going against my own beliefs? I didn't know how the morning-after pill worked, or what it did – the doctor never explained it to me – so I didn't know if I was crossing the line by taking it. Was I snuffing out a life that had already been created? Or was I just preventing a potential life from being created in the first place? I thought about spitting the pill out again, but then I thought that if I actually *was* pregnant, and some of the medication had already entered my bloodstream, then it might have harmful effects on the baby. So I swallowed it. But it didn't feel right.

After that they sent me to talk to a counsellor. The counselling was meant to be optional but it didn't feel optional – it felt like just one more horrible thing they were making me go through. When I went in to see her I just felt like she was pissed off at me because I wasn't giving the responses she wanted. She was trying to get me to open up, but it was the day after I'd been raped, I'd had a hard enough time telling the police what body part went where, and I knew my family were sitting right outside the door (they couldn't hear me, but it was still really off-putting), so she didn't get much out of me. I was supposed to go back and see her once a week as part of my treatment, but I didn't want to have anything to do with it, so I arranged to see my school counsellor instead. I knew there'd always be some really important thing I had to do at school that would get me out of seeing the counsellor, so that way I could skip the whole counselling thing altogether.

After I'd finished with the counsellor I was allowed to leave the hospital, but I still hadn't reached the end of the process. Kellie wanted to take me back to Kogarah for more questioning.

I was getting to the end of my tether. It was getting late in the day, I hadn't had any real sleep, and I hadn't eaten, plus I was still in shock, I'd been stuck like a pincushion at the hospital and I still hadn't taken in what had happened to me the night before. Kellie took me to Maccas and got me a feed, and I felt a little bit better after I'd had something to eat. After that, we went on to the next stage: taking my formal statement.

When we got to Kogarah I was taken to an interview room so Kellie could take my statement, which would be recorded on video. Next door to the interview room was a second small room which was full of technical equipment. They explained to me that there'd be two tapes made – one was red, and it would be sealed until the day of the trial. This was so no one could tamper with it and no one could say that evidence had been added in or edited out. It was strictly a record of what I'd said. The other tape was yellow, and that was the tape we would use for evidence. Copies of this tape would be sent to all the different people investigating my case.

After they showed me all the recording equipment they

took me into a room that looked like a small lounge room – it had a coffee table, two blue couches, little microphones and cameras all over the room – and sat me down with a police officer called Sandy Goodfellow. Then the questioning started again.

People had been asking me the same questions all day, and now I was answering the same questions again, in really graphic detail.

I'd say something like: 'And then he stuck his dick in me.'

And Sandy would ask, 'Do you have another word for "dick"?'

So I'd have to say, 'Penis.'

'And where did he put his penis?'

'In my privates.'

'Do you have another word for that?'

'Vagina.'

She wanted me to use the correct terminology for everything, and using those words made me feel incredibly uncomfortable. I was only fourteen and immature – I'd lived a sheltered life up until that night – and I went to an all-girls' school where if someone said anything that sounded even remotely sexual or taboo, we all made fun of them. We didn't talk about sex, and if we *did*, we didn't use those words. So having to talk about all that stuff in front of a police officer (not to mention all those cameras!) was incredibly hard for me. I *hated* every minute of it.

The questioning went on for what felt like hours. I sat there talking and talking; drawing little diagrams; answering questions a hundred times. All I wanted to do was go home and sleep. Eventually they decided they'd asked me enough questions for one day, and they were going to let me go home. There was just one more thing they wanted me to do for them: they asked if they could take my undies. I was still wearing the undies I'd put on after I got back to Kerry's house, so I guess they were hoping to find more evidence. You wouldn't think, after everything I'd been through, that I'd care about giving up my undies. But I did.

'Okay,' Sandy said, after I'd let them take my undies away in an evidence bag. 'We're going to continue the statement on Monday. Can you come back Monday?'

Finally there was an upside to this whole nightmare! Monday was a school day, and making a statement was a *great* excuse to get out of school.

'Sure,' I said, 'I'll come Monday.'

It had been an incredibly long, gruelling day, and I was desperate to get to sleep. But even when I was safe at home, tucked up in my own bed, I couldn't sleep properly. I was too scared. My bedroom was on the ground floor and I woke up in the middle of the night terrified that the boys were going to come after me. I had to grab all my bedclothes off the bed and go and sleep upstairs. Even my own home didn't feel safe anymore. It was horrible.

On Monday I went back to the police station to finish making my statement. This questioning wasn't as easy as the first one – not that that had been easy. They asked me all the same questions that I'd been asked two days before – but this time they wanted to know everything down to the tiniest detail. They'd ask me things like: 'When he grabbed you into the room, did he grab you with his right hand or left hand?'

As if I could remember that! But on the odd occasion I did remember. 'He grabbed me with his right hand.'

'And what hand of yours did he grab? Did he grab your right hand or your left hand?'

It was silly. I couldn't remember those things. It's not the sort of thing you pay attention to when it's happening to you. But they kept asking ridiculous questions, over and over again, so I had to keep trying to answer them – and the more questions they asked me, the more I felt like I was under attack. It's hard not to feel like they're doubting you when they question every little thing you say. The longer it went on, the more tense and angry I got. Eventually I felt like I was ready to snap – or just break down and cry. I started back-talking and becoming a little bit rude. After I'd said something particularly sarky, Sandy said, 'I think we should take a break.'

They switched the cameras off and Sandy took me aside. 'Now just calm down, okay?' she said. 'I want you to remember the jury are going to be watching this. They don't want to see some bratty teen going off at a police officer and being rude and sarcastic. I know this is really hard, and it seems like we're being too tough on you. But believe me, when we get to trial, the lawyers for the other side are going to be a whole lot harder on you than we are.'

I wasn't ready to listen to her. I just thought she didn't believe me and that was why she was giving me such a hard time. It didn't occur to me that she was just trying to prepare me for what was to come.

My cousin Paul had come with me to keep me company while I made my statement. He wasn't in the room with me – he waited outside – but without him I don't know how I would have got through the rest of the day. The police were being incredibly serious, and my mum and my nan (who'd also come along) were completely out of their depth. Paul was the only one who seemed relaxed. The two of us joked about how bad the coffee was and how the person who'd made my coffee was really hopeless at it. I complained so loudly I think the officer heard me, and Paul said I'd probably scarred her for life by insulting her coffee-making skills. It wasn't particularly funny, but it calmed me down and brought me back to reality.

Somehow, I got through the rest of the day and completed my statement. By the end of it I was completely drained. I didn't want to see anyone or talk to anyone. I never wanted to see anybody ever again. I just wanted to hide in my room until it was all over.

When I got home I went to my room and sat in my cupboard, which was something I only did when I was really frantically upset, wishing and wishing that my dad was still alive. I'd started hiding in small places after my Dad died –

partly because I wanted to be where no one could find me, but also because I needed to be somewhere small and private where I could sit and think. I missed Dad so much and I needed him so much. If he'd been alive I could've told him everything that had happened, and he would have made me feel like everything was going to be okay. But he wasn't there, so I kept holding onto my teddy – the one that he'd given me when I was little – and playing with the locket that I'd been given after he died, thinking about him and wondering what he'd do if he knew about all this. Wondering if he'd be proud of me. Wondering if he'd be angry at me. Wondering if he'd be ashamed of me . . .

Ashamed. That's how I felt. Dirty, and ashamed. I kept looking at my body and thinking, *How could these people have done this to me?* I couldn't wrap my head around the fact that someone had been inside of me. Someone had been there and I didn't want them to be and I couldn't do anything about it. I just sat there and cried.

Finally I went to bed, and cried myself to sleep.

# 6

# Fallout

EVERYTHING CHANGED AFTER THE rapes, for me and for my family.

When something like this happens, sometimes it can be easier to talk about it to strangers than it is to talk to your own family. That's how it was for me. Talking to the police hadn't been *easy*, but for them it was all part of their job, something they dealt with every day. And for me, talking to them was a way of making it all go away. I could hand it over to them and let *them* deal with it.

But my family were just about impossible to talk to. They'd never had to deal with anything like this before, and they didn't know how to respond to it at all. They wanted to help me, but they were dealing with their own feelings about what had happened, and so I just felt like, whoa, I know you guys are taking it really hard right now but can you take it hard somewhere else? Especially on the first day, all my family were in my face the whole time. They were trying to be supportive, but there are some members of my family I can only take in small doses, and when all of them were gathered in one room, at a really stressful time, it just made everything harder, not easier.

My mother came down from Port Macquarie to be with me, and the first thing she said when she got off the plane was: 'I'm sick of everybody thinking I'm a bad parent. I'm here now, aren't I?' I couldn't help feeling she was only there to keep up appearances, so people wouldn't think badly of her. It had nothing to do with me and how *I* was feeling.

My mother had post-natal depression when I was born. She doesn't remember the first three months of me being alive, so we never formed any initial bond, and things never really got any better between us. There's just something about our personalities that makes us clash. We couldn't be in the same room together for long without fighting. I do love my mum, it's just that we're not close – at all.

My older brother Brendan was only three or four months old when Mum fell pregnant with me. She has epilepsy and her body chemicals hadn't returned to normal after the first pregnancy. I grew quickly and got too big for her, so I was induced a month early. Mum's post-natal depression was so bad she couldn't look after me properly, so we all moved in with my nan so she could help. Nan told me that there were a few times when she actually thought I was in danger. The first night she was home with me my mother started freaking out and pushed my bassinette so it rolled across the room and out the door. Nan had to rescue me and then try to calm her down again so she could convince her to feed me. Mum doesn't remember any of that. It wasn't her fault.

Because my mum wasn't really there for me for the first three months I bonded with my dad instead. It was Dad who looked after me and Dad was the one I went to when something was wrong or I needed something. He was a great dad, and the two of us were really close. I adored him.

I used to help Dad around the house and watch him while he did things. I remember sitting and watching him while he was working on our boat. It had a registration number on the side and I said, 'Don't worry 2 4 7 8, my daddy's going to fix you,' which he thought was very funny. I remember helping him wash our dog, Foxy, in the wheelbarrow. And I remember once I pretended to be sick so I could stay home from school with him, and the two of us made sultana cookies and I tried to eat all of them before my brothers came home. He loved CCs and I wouldn't eat them because I said they were too spicy, and he always tried to convince me they weren't spicy at all. I love spicy food now.

I don't really have memories of my mum from when I was

very little. I only remember my dad. Both my parents were in the fire brigade, but I only remember my dad being in it when I was small. I remember Mum being in the fire brigade when I was older. But when I was really little she didn't really seem to register.

Three weeks before my seventh birthday my dad died. He got cancer: a brain tumour right in the middle of his brain so they couldn't operate and all they could do was give him chemotherapy. The technology for cancer treatment wasn't as good then as it is now, so he didn't really stand much of a chance. He didn't last long after he was diagnosed.

When he died, things went massively downhill between me and my mum. We fought about stupid things – we were a seven-year-old and a 27-year-old fighting about stuff that you wouldn't think anyone would be fighting about. It was so immature and so stupid but we just couldn't get along.

Not long after he died, my mum went to England for six weeks as a companion for my gran (my nan's mother). While she was away I stayed with my nan, and she sent me to Sylvania Primary School where they discovered that I had a reading and writing disability. After my dad died I'd gotten completely blocked and just stopped learning. No one at my old school, Sussex Inlet Primary, had actually noticed, but at Sylvania they said they could put me in a program to pick up my reading and writing skills. After my mum came back from England I went back to live with her and my brothers and sister, but things only got worse between us, and eventually it was decided I should go and live with my nan for a while. It was just meant to be a bit of a break, but I ended up staying there for the next eleven years.

My mother is a restless spirit. She's always moved around a lot. When I was about ten she moved back to Sylvania and moved in with us for a while – it was a big house – and she decided that I should rejoin the family and start moving around with them again. It was a complete disaster. I'd been with Nan for about three years and by then I was used to a different home life. I had a really religious upbringing, all my needs were met, and I'd been happy with my nan. I wasn't used to there being no routine, I wasn't used to fights, and having to argue to get things that I wanted. I wasn't used to having to share everything with my brothers and sister. I had toys that I'd managed to keep from when I was really young, toys that my dad had given me, and they just got trashed because they didn't mean as much to them as they did to me. That's just what brothers and sisters do, but I wasn't used to it. So it was hard – I couldn't get along with them and I couldn't get along with my mum. She was dating as well and I didn't cope well with that – I hated her boyfriends. And so eventually my nan said, 'That's it, I'm picking you up and taking you back home to live with me.' So that was that.

Because my mum moved around so much – she lived in Mollymook, in Sussex Inlet, in Port Macquarie, all over the place (she's now in Queensland) – I never really had a chance to build any sort of relationship with her. My nan's always been more of a mother to me than my actual mum ever has. Even now, if I need help, I'll call my nan. If I have to put somebody down as my next of kin, it's my nan's name that I write. Nan has said to me that she feels more like a mother than a grandmother to me, and I feel the same way about her, which means that my mum seems more like a really annoying big sister who likes to fight with me, so we never did form a bond.

But in spite of all that, Mum flew down to be with me after the rapes. And as soon as she arrived the two of us fought like cat and dog, just like we did when I was younger. Those first few days it felt like Mum and Nan were constantly ganging up on me, with Mum acting as the ringleader and Nan just going with the flow. Mum told me that I had to apologise to my nan for going to the party because I lied about where I was and that if I hadn't been there it would never have happened. What my mother meant was, if I'd answered my nan correctly when she asked me, 'Where are you going?' then none of this would have happened, because Nan would of course have said, 'You're fourteen – you're not going, you're staying at home.' But that's not how it came across to me. It sounded like my mum was saying, 'You should never have gone to this party. If you hadn't gone to this party, you wouldn't have gotten raped. Therefore, the whole thing was your fault.'

That is *so* the wrong thing to say to a rape victim. I didn't want to hear that the rape was my fault. Sure, I shouldn't have been there. But at the same time, I could've been running down Oxford Street buck naked and that still didn't give anyone the right to rape me. Yet it felt like my mother was saying it was all my fault. And whenever Mum or Nan tried to talk to me about what had happened I felt like they were angry at me, or they were picking on me, or using what had happened as a weapon against me. And that just made me angry.

A few days after the rapes, Kerry rang up to see if I was okay. I would have liked to talk to Kerry and try to deal with things my own way, which would have involved yelling at her a lot and then trying to explain to her that the rapes really happened, and that if she kept hanging around with those guys, eventually they were going to screw her over too. Instead, Mum grabbed the phone and told her, 'You're an unsavoury little girl!' and hung up on her.

Mum stayed for about a week in the end. I kept telling her she had to go home because it was my little brother's birthday and she couldn't possibly miss it, but really I just didn't want her around.

She had no idea how difficult she made it for me. I didn't really know how she felt about what had happened – I didn't know if she was angry at me, if she hated me for it, if she believed me or not. Whenever I tried to ask her about it, we couldn't have a calm, sensible discussion, we'd just end up having these big theatrical scenes. I guess it was her way of coping. But it didn't help me much.

It was a relief when she finally went home.

THINGS BECAME MORE DIFFICULT between me and my nan, too.

At the beginning when we were dealing with the police and going to the hospital she insisted on coming with me, even though I would have preferred to go on my own. At the police station I told her I didn't want her or my grandfather to come in with me, but she wasn't having a bar of it.

'I can't leave you to go through all this by yourself,' she said. 'You're too young. You need somebody with you.'

She didn't like it when she had to wait outside the room when I had my examination and gave my statement, but that's the only way I could handle it. I find it easier to deal with stressful situations if I can do it on my own.

The morning-after pill gave her a lot of angst. She was with me in the hospital when the doctor gave it to me, and ordinarily she would have jumped right in and told me not to take it because it went against her beliefs. But that day she wasn't sure what to do: if she told me not to take the pill and I *did* get pregnant it would make a bad situation a million times worse. At the age of fourteen I'd be faced with some terrible choices: should I have the baby, then give it up for adoption? Or keep it, and be reminded every day of the rapists? How would a baby affect my education and my future? Not taking the pill could ruin my life, and she didn't want to risk that, so she let me take it. But I know she felt bad about it. She ended up going to confession about it later.

Things changed dramatically between us after the rapes. Nan had trust issues because I had lied to her about where I was, and I had issues with her because I didn't think that she understood what I was going through and she wasn't sympathetic towards me. She thought she knew what was best for me but she hadn't been in the situation herself so I had no time for her opinion and that caused nothing but fights. I was always full of tension, so every conversation turned into an argument, no matter how innocently it started. If someone asked me more than two questions in a row they got their head bitten off. And it didn't matter what questions they were. It didn't matter if it was, 'Have you put your school bag in your room?' and 'Where are your school shoes?' If someone dared to ask me what I did with my school dress, that was it. It was all on. Because I felt like everybody was in my face the whole time and I'd had enough of it. And unfortunately, my nan copped most of that.

Even though we were constantly fighting, she kept trying to talk to me about what had happened. I really think she was trying to help. But I just wished she'd leave the whole topic alone. Just to put this in perspective, imagine telling your parents (and that's what my grandparents were like, my parents) about the most intimate details of your sex life. It's not exactly dinner conversation. I didn't even *have* a sex life, but that's how much of an invasion the questions felt to me. And it wasn't just that I didn't want to talk to her about something that was private. I didn't want her to have to deal with the reality of what had happened to me. I didn't want her to hear about how I was raped. I didn't want her to hear about how I had a boy on top of me, forcing his penis into me. I didn't want her to hear how a boy had his tongue down my throat or how another boy had slapped me and told me he was going to stab me. I didn't want to tell her that. I didn't even want to tell my friends that. I just wanted to keep it to myself – I never wanted to talk about it ever again.

I'd had a good relationship with my nan before all this happened. We didn't fight much and I'd always done what I was told. I'd been basically a pretty good kid. But after the rapes, an element of distrust and suspicion and resentment crept in and undermined everything. It was kind of a vicious circle: Nan didn't trust me anymore, I didn't feel supported, Nan found me harder and harder to deal with, I felt more and more like I didn't have a home. We fought, we couldn't understand each other, we couldn't communicate. Our whole relationship began to unravel. And maybe that would have happened anyway – maybe that's part of being a teenager – but to me it felt like the fourteenth of June was the day when our relationship started to go wrong.

\* \* \*

ONE OF THE MOST difficult things about a traumatic experience like rape is that even when it's over, it's not over. I wasn't prepared for that; nobody warned me. Nobody told me anything.

There isn't a manual for rape victims warning you what to expect. There should be, but there isn't. The counsellors and doctors had told my grandparents what to expect – that I might have anxiety attacks, disordered sleep, flashbacks, and a whole lot of other things – but nobody thought to tell the one person who really needed to know: me. Maybe they thought I was too young to be told or maybe they thought my grandparents would fill me in, but somebody really should have told me what to expect, and no one did.

People underestimate what victims are capable of being told. I was under-age, so maybe my grandparents had to be told on my behalf. But there was no communication whatsoever between the three of us – it was wrong to tell them and not me. I'm the one who's going to have the anxiety attacks. I'm the one who's going to have the flashbacks. I'm the one who's feeling all the emotions. I'm the one who really needs to know, not them.

I'd been given all sorts of brochures to read, but they hadn't given me what I needed. I wanted concrete information: *you might have flashbacks, and they're going to be like this, and this is what you do about them.* Or: *this is what happens when you have an anxiety attack. It's all right – don't rush off; don't get a cardiograph. You can manage this on your own, and here's how.*

But there was none of that. Instead it was: *we think you're going to go through this and we're going to try and give you advice, but really, we don't know. We're lost. We're clueless. But we think if you do this, you're going to be okay* and *If you'd like to apply for a counsellor, please send these forms in.* There were no tips for how to deal with it yourself, in your own way. There was no little paragraph underneath saying *If you hate counsellors and would rather handle this yourself then you can do this.* There were no other options – it was a counsellor or nothing.

I'm the kind of person who'd rather work things out for themselves, and that's why I have a bit of a problem with counsellors. Kevin Bale, one of the policemen who worked on my case, told Nan one day he thought it was a given I was going to have a breakdown at some stage, but I never did. That's because I've always had the ability to step away from myself and look at my own thoughts and actions and think okay, why am I feeling this? Where is this leading to? I'm my own analyst, and that's what saved me. But some information would have helped too.

What I wanted was a clear, honest, straightforward account from someone who'd actually been there, telling the truth about what happened to them, so I could have a sense of what to expect and how to handle it. Now, I know not all victims are the same, and they're not all going to have the same reactions and responses. Every rape victim has her own story to tell, and her own way of surviving. Other rape victims might not experience any of the things that happened to me. All

I know is, it would have helped me to know what someone else had been through, and to know that you can handle it, and it does get better.

So here's what happened to me.

When something traumatic happens to you, your body reacts in all sorts of unexpected ways. The nightmares started the first night; for a long time afterwards I'd wake up terrified because I thought the boys were coming after me, or that I was back in that room with them again.

I was haunted by dreams and nightmares about babies too: I dreamed that I *had* got pregnant after all, and that I'd lost the baby somehow, and then I'd experience these terrible feelings of guilt and grief about having left the baby on the bus.

I have psoriasis, which gets worse whenever I'm stressed. After the rapes, my skin broke out in red blotches all over my body. It got so bad I had to get UV treatment for it, which involved standing in a sunbox for three minutes every day. I ended up with a pretty good tan, but I could have done without the psoriasis – and the stress.

I also experienced other symptoms I'd never felt before: an intense pain, like knives stabbing into my body. The first time I felt it I was terrified; I thought I was having a heart attack. But then it went away again, and over time I discovered that the way to deal with it was to take slow, deep breaths – not easy when it feels like you're being stabbed – and try to just calm down and relax until it went away again. I had these symptoms for six months without knowing what they were, and the whole time I was frightened I was going to drop dead of a heart attack. Eventually one day it came up in conversation that I 'might' get anxiety attacks.

'Oh really?' I said. 'I *might* get anxiety attacks? What are they like?'

Six months too late, Nan filled me in. It was quite a relief to know my heart wasn't about to explode.

At first it seemed like the anxiety attacks just came out of the blue, but gradually I began to realise there was a pattern to them. They were sometimes triggered by things that reminded me of that night – especially smells. The scent of vanilla was one trigger, because I'd been wearing a vanilla-flavoured deodorant. A particular kind of male BO triggered it too – not plain ordinary sweaty-guy BO, but BO flavoured by Pakistani cooking. If I saw a dark-coloured Skyline on the street I'd freak, because I'd be afraid it was them. And I got nauseous whenever I saw baklava, because the day I was giving my statement to the police, Nan and Mum had gone out and bought some as a treat, and it was so sweet and disgusting I just about threw up, and I couldn't stand the sight of it afterwards.

But sometimes there wasn't any obvious trigger. I'd have an anxiety attack, or a flashback, and I'd just have to try and deal with it. It could happen at any time: sitting in class, brushing my teeth, sitting in front of the TV. My chest would tighten and I'd get this horrible pain, or I'd suddenly have a flashback to something that had happened that night, and I'd have to try and act as if nothing was happening.

I was also still on the medication I'd been prescribed to stop me from getting HIV. I had to take that for six weeks, and for a while there I was completely drugged up. It's a hard medication to take. It makes you tired so you don't want to do anything. It completely changed my personality – I went from being a noisy, energetic person to being sleepy and quiet. It worked – I didn't get HIV, or any other STDs – but I had to deal with the side effects of strong medication as well as everything else.

I needed to find a way to cope with everything I was feeling, and one of the ways I found was bulimia.

I remember once when I was very little, only about two, I was playing with my brother when my parents weren't around, and I started to choke on a two-cent piece. I remember being really frightened because I thought I was going to die and there was nothing I could do about it. And my brother could see that I was choking but he didn't know what to do, so he punched me in the stomach and I had such a strong reaction I threw up the thing I was choking on. I don't know if my parents ever knew about it; my brother probably wouldn't remember it either. But I remember it very clearly.

Ever since then I've had these muscles in my belly that let me do all kinds of really gross tricks – and I can also throw up at will. When I first started doing it, it took quite an effort, but once I got into the habit it actually became quite difficult to keep food down.

Some people become bulimic because they want to get

thin, but that wasn't why I did it. (I did get thinner, but for me that was just a side-effect.) I did it because I wanted to hurt my body.

It started because I needed to react to what had happened to me, and I didn't have a way to react. Crying's not my thing. I've never really liked telling other people how I feel because I'm afraid they're going to think I'm full of it. I needed to do something to express how I was feeling, but at the same time I wanted it to be a secret. I needed a way of expressing how I was feeling that no one else would know about, something that was just for me. Bulimia seemed like a solution to my problem.

Drinking a lot of liquid was the key: if I had a big soft drink or a lot of milk with a meal, it'd come up really easily. I completely reversed the way my body worked: if I was hungry I wouldn't have hunger pains, I'd feel great; and if my stomach was full I wouldn't feel satisfied, I'd feel sick. Once I started, it quickly got out of control. I couldn't eat without having to go somewhere and throw up, and once I started I couldn't stop until I'd thrown up everything in my stomach and I was dry-retching. Once I had an empty stomach again I'd feel better, and then I could stop. I threw up so much I started having dizzy spells. I'd feel light-headed and dizzy, and sometimes I'd even faint. But if anyone saw me looking dizzy I always told them I was sick – I never told them I was bulimic.

I knew it was a problem and I did try to get help. I went to a lot of different doctors but no one seemed to know what

I should do. One place I tried said they only dealt with anorexics; everyone I spoke to kept referring me to someone else. In the end I gave up.

After a while, bulimia wasn't enough anymore. I couldn't stop throwing up, but it didn't make me feel better. At the end of one particularly bad day when I was in Year 10, when I felt like I'd fought with everybody and I had absolutely no one left to turn to and everything was pushing me to the point where I thought I was going to snap, I decided to try cutting myself. I cut a line on my leg with a pair of scissors so it bled. The surprising thing is it didn't hurt at all. If I'd cut myself accidentally, that would have hurt. But when I did it deliberately, it just felt satisfying. Up until the moment I cut myself it felt like I was going nuts, but then the blade went in and I saw the blood and I instantly felt a sense of satisfaction, as if everything that was going wrong had now been put back in its place, and then for however long it took to heal whenever I felt the scab brush against my clothing I felt that secret satisfaction. It was like a drug.

One of my friends did it, too. I spotted it straight away at school, and I confronted her about it. 'You've been cutting yourself, haven't you? I know, because I do it too.' It became a private joke between us: we called ourselves the Slice 'n' Dice Club. Whenever we saw each other we'd ask, 'Slice 'n' dice lately?' and then we'd talk about whatever was going on in our lives. It was great talking to her about it because I always knew she'd understand. I could say to her, 'I cut myself again the other day and it was so satisfying.' And she'd say, 'You know what? The other day I almost got an artery and it scared the crap out of me, but it still felt really good.' If we'd told anybody else what we were doing they would have gone off at us and said, 'Why are you doing such a stupid thing? That's disgusting! Stop it at once!' She was the one person who got it. She understood the impulse to cut and she understood how good it felt afterwards, so when I talked to her I knew she'd know where I was coming from. And the more we talked about things, the less we cut ourselves.

But I always knew it was there as an option if everything got on top of me. It was my safety valve.

# 7

# The whispers
# of bitchy girls

A COUPLE OF WEEKS after I was raped I was listening to the radio one morning before school. My grandparents listened to talkback radio, and there was a debate on about the Skaf case. (Brothers Mohammed and Bilal Skaf were the ringleaders of a group of young men who picked up and gang-raped a number of girls. In July 2002 – just a few weeks after I was raped – the brothers were convicted, and Bilal Skaf was sentenced to 55 years in jail. The case caused a media frenzy.) This woman called up in defence of the Skaf boys. She said that women who got raped deserved to get raped and wanted to be raped and it was their fault because of what they were wearing. She said if girls went out properly covered up then people wouldn't look at them as sex objects and there wouldn't be any rapes. And I just wanted to call her up and tell her off. I wanted to abuse the living daylights out of her. But my nan wouldn't let me do it. She kept telling me, 'Just wait, don't do it. After your case you can do it,' thinking that it would only be a couple of weeks. (In fact it took three years.) So I didn't call the radio station and give that woman a serve. I just went to school as usual. But for the rest of the day all I could think about was what she'd said and how wrong and unfair it was. This woman had basically accused me of being promiscuous, when I was *so* not promiscuous. I was fourteen. I'd never kissed a guy before. I looked like a baby hippo. I had serious body issues. I was self-conscious, I was shy. I was only talkative around my friends. I didn't have much confidence whatsoever and suddenly these guys were cracking onto me and trying to do stuff to me and I couldn't think of a way to escape. And yet this woman was saying that everything that had happened was my fault because of the way I was dressed. How could I not take it personally? It just made me so mad that a woman could say something like that. It was like she was backstabbing her own gender.

But what I discovered when I went back to school is that if you think you're going to get support and understanding from other women, forget it. I went to an all-girls' school, and when it comes to being judgmental, bitchy and cruel, girls leave guys for dead. For me, going back to school was probably the hardest part of the whole experience. It was like walking into a lions' den every single day.

The Monday night after I'd finished giving my statement to the police, Mum, Nan and I had a discussion about when I should go back to school. Mum was convinced I had to go back straight away and that it was the best thing for me. I knew I wasn't ready to go back. I'd spent days telling my story to people, over and over, in excruciating detail. I'd been raped, traumatised, examined, injected and interrogated. I was still dealing with what had happened to me, and all I really wanted was to be left alone. But my grandparents and my mum decided for me: I was going back to school.

What was I going to tell my friends? They were all going to want to know why I hadn't been at school on Monday. I didn't know what to tell them. I didn't know how to answer their questions. I thought maybe I should tell them before I went back so they'd understand, but the thought of ringing them all up and telling them, one by one, was just more than I could handle.

But when I got to school the next morning I found out that everybody already knew about it because someone had got on the train and told everybody. I wasn't sure *what* they knew. But they knew.

There were rumours going around that I wasn't raped at all, I'd just made it up; that I'd been sleeping with the boys and my grandparents found out about it so I decided to *tell* everyone I was raped; that I was pregnant; that one or two other girls had held a gun to my head; that I'd been stabbed and I had all these ugly big stitches under my school uniform. Everybody had heard a different story and everybody had an opinion about it. Everywhere I went, girls were staring at me and whispering and making comments. Even before the rapes I was awkward and self-conscious; walking into school afterwards and having to cope with everybody staring at me and talking about me was one of the hardest things I've ever had to do.

My grandparents had decided we needed to tell the school, so they told the principal, and then she got all the teachers together and told them. And I knew exactly when she told them, because my roll-call room was right next to the staff room, and as each and every one of them walked out I saw them glance in at me, and then when they realised I could see them they'd look away really quickly, and I was thinking, okay, she just told you all didn't she? All right. Let the special treatment begin.

There was one teacher called Mrs M who really helped me. She ran the Special Ed program – I was involved in it because of my reading and writing disability. One lesson a day, or a couple of times a week, depending on how much we needed it, we'd go to the library and the Special Ed teachers would help us catch up on the day's work. I think I spent most of that first week just hanging out with Mrs M in the library. She'd let me do my thing, or she'd help me get to my classroom if

I needed it. I think all the Special Ed teachers must have spent a lot of time thinking about ways they could help me, because they were really great. I didn't get a lot of support from the school or my fellow students, but Mrs M was great. For me, she's still up on a pedestal.

My year coordinator got my entire year together and told them what had happened. It was supposed to stop the rumours but it was just incredibly embarrassing. I refused to be in the room while she did it – I went and sat in the office so I wouldn't have to listen to it. I didn't want to sit through someone else telling my story, and watching everyone's reactions, and then having them turn around to stare at me.

My school was a girls' school, but there was a boys' school in a nearby suburb, and in Year 11 the two schools joined up at a seniors' college. The principal of the boys' school told all of his students what had happened too. So it wasn't just everyone at my school who knew about me. All the boys knew as well.

One of the things that drove me crazy about all this was the fact that it was impossible to control the information. When you're raped, your privacy gets violated at the same time as your body. But after the rapes, my privacy kept on getting violated, over and over and over again – by the police and the hospital, and then by other kids and the school. And later on, when we went to court, it got picked up by the media, and people I'd never even met knew all kinds of stuff about me, half of which was wrong, and they had opinions about me, and there was absolutely nothing I could do about it. So I just had to try and survive it.

I know the school were trying to do their best for me, but they were just like everyone else – police, parents, doctors. They'd made up their minds about what they thought should happen, and I didn't get a say. They just told me, 'This is how we're going to handle it, because we think this is the right way to do it.' Too bad if I had a different opinion. It was my reputation, my body, my life. But nobody ever seemed interested in what *I* thought should happen.

I accept it was necessary for them to lay the rumours to rest. But they didn't ask me what I wanted them to say. They didn't ask me if I wanted the boys' school told. (I *definitely* didn't.) They could have asked the girls to respect my privacy and not ask me about it all the time – they didn't. And once they'd made the announcement, the teachers could have supported me when they saw the other girls harassing me. But they did nothing.

My friends didn't know how to deal with it. I had a group of five really close friends, and when they first heard about what happened they all came over to my house and made a fuss of me. They bought me a box of flowers and a little black toy puppy – it was so cute – and some of my favourite Dream white chocolate. (I could never eat white chocolate again after that. It was just one more thing that became associated with the rapes in my head. I still can't eat it.) They also gave me a card saying, 'Dear Tegan, we're really sorry this has happened to you but if you ever need anybody to talk to, we're here for you.' And that was probably the best way they could've put it. They were trying to be nice, the only way they knew how – it wasn't a situation any of us really knew how to deal with. But I gradually began to suspect that not all of them actually believed me.

My group had little books that we used for writing letters to each other. We all had five books, and each book would be shared with just one friend, so you'd write a letter to your friend and then she'd write one back to you. These books were like long private conversations which just happened to be written down, so as soon as you looked in one you could immediately see who'd been bitching about who. They were supposed to be private, but . . . you know what fourteen-year-olds are like. And one day I picked up a book that belonged to my best friend at the time. It was a book that she shared with another of my friends, and I was just flicking through it because I knew there was going to be juicy information in it about someone . . . and there were about four or five pages dedicated to whether I was lying about being raped. My best friend. They thought maybe I'd had sex with the boys and then decided it was a bad idea afterwards and come up with the rape story. And one of them said, 'I don't believe it happened at all, as if anyone would touch her.' It was just common bitchy girl stuff, but I was absolutely devastated. So I confronted them about it – in fact I really went off the deep end at them. I told them I really had been raped, and if they wanted proof, what about all the tablets I was taking? (I was on medication for HIV and my friends had all seen me taking the tablets.) It turned into a real issue between me and my friends. For about a month afterwards, every time the subject came up I'd challenge them, 'Well, gee, guys, do you believe me or not?' And they all said yes, of course they believed me. But I reckon out of my five closest friends, only one or two of them really believed me. The others took a while to be convinced. It's hard to stay really close to people when they've doubted you like that, and that was the beginning of the end for me and that group of friends. I stayed close to one of the girls, and I still see her today. But I began to drift away from the others, and it wasn't long before I found new friends with very different interests.

Of course, it wasn't just my own friends who had doubts about me. Everyone in the school had an opinion about whether I was telling the truth or not. Girls I'd never even spoken to would come up to me and make comments about it. And one of the main reasons a lot of the girls at my school thought I was lying was because of my weight. I've always had problems with my weight and when I was fourteen I was heavy – I weighed about 115 kilos. There were a lot of girls at my school – including some of my friends – who thought that I wasn't pretty or popular enough to get raped. In reality it's not just the pretty and popular girls that get raped. You don't have to be a supermodel. Average girls get raped too. It's not as though potential rapists are out there targeting a particular type of girl because they think she's hot; all she has to be is female. That's all. It's the only requirement. You don't need boobs. You don't need pretty hair. You don't need pretty eyes. You just need to have a vagina. That's all a rapist needs. But a lot of girls at my school were acting like it was some kind of beauty contest.

One girl came up to me and said, 'Do you think you got raped? Who'd rape you?!' And the next thing I remember I was slamming her into a toilet wall saying to her, 'If you ever say that to me again I'm going to smash you.' And my friends had to run in after me and pull me off her. I was so mad I was shaking, and my friends were like, 'Whoa . . . !' They'd never seen me do that before. I think I scared everybody that day, including myself. But it just kept happening, because people kept coming up and making comments to me, and every time someone said something I'd lash out. I couldn't help myself.

One of the boys from the seniors' college came up to me at Miranda train station. The station was being renovated and half the platform was blocked, so it took a long time for everybody to get past. And he said, in the loudest voice possible, 'Hey, that's the girl that got raped!' I couldn't believe it. And even though he was twice my height, twice my size, I charged him. I threw him up against a wall and chucked him to the ground and said, 'If you disrespect a girl like that again you're not going to have anything to reproduce.' My friend Sarah had to drag me off him, yelling, 'Leave him, Tegan! He's not worth it!' The boy just slunk away – and when I finally started at the seniors' college I didn't hear a peep from him. The whole time I was there, every time he walked past me he kept his head down.

Before the rapes there's no way I would have chucked someone up against a wall – I wouldn't have had the strength to do it, even if I wanted to. But after the rapes I was so violent and angry and unpredictable it really started to scare my friends. I just wanted to lash out at people because I couldn't believe how unsympathetic they were being towards me. And it wasn't that I *wanted* their sympathy; all I wanted was for everybody to shut up and get the hell over it. But people wouldn't leave the subject alone.

Not everyone was unsympathetic. There were people who really stuck by me. I knew one girl who was friendly with both me and Kerry. And she found herself in a pretty awkward position, because she knew what Kerry was like, and even though she liked her, she knew a bit about the guys she'd gotten involved with and so she knew something really bad probably had happened. This girl was one of the few people who believed me from the word go. She knew I wouldn't make up something like that just for the hell of it. I never had to explain myself to her or justify myself or give evidence to prove that I was telling the truth. She just believed me, and it was such a relief. She didn't go in for big dramatic scenes, but when people around her were making comments and saying horrible things about me, she'd always stand up for me. And not just when I was there either – she stood up for me when she didn't have to, and when it would have been a lot easier for her to say nothing at all. I really admire her for that.

Another friend, Ann, was a true friend. I'd known her since Year 6 and she was one of my group of five friends. She always believed me – she never thought I'd made it up. She was a bit of a tomboy, so she wasn't the kind of girl who went in for deep and meaningfuls. If you needed someone to talk to, she was hopeless. In the whole time I've known her, I've only ever had one hug from her. But she was an honest friend, she was easy to be with, she wasn't fake and she wasn't nasty. We're still friends today. (The hug thing's become a private joke between us – whenever I see her I'll say 'Awkward hug' and then we'll hug each other like we're hugging a dead animal.)

What I really needed was someone I could talk to, someone who'd really understand what I was going through, but I didn't have anyone. I couldn't talk to my grandparents – obviously. I couldn't talk to my friends, either because they were like Ann and weren't much good at talking about their feelings, or because they hadn't initially believed me, so it was hard for me to really trust them again. I felt like everyone around me was either doubting me or judging me. No one who was close to me had been through anything even remotely like this, so there was no one I could talk to who really knew what it was like.

The school had a counsellor and I had regular appointments with her. But they weren't much help. In my opinion the problem with counsellors is they treat all their patients as if they're case studies. They listen to what you have to say and then they think, all right, I'm going to turn to page 24 of *Child Psychology:* What Happens to Rape Victims. I'm not a textbook – I'm an individual and I want to be treated like one. So I didn't have anything to say to the counsellor. She probably thought it was because I was traumatised and upset, but it wasn't. I just didn't want to hear what was on page 24 of the textbook.

Eventually one day I'd had enough and I said, 'What would you know? You've never had this happen to you.'

'How do you know this hasn't happened to me?' she asked.

'Well, has it?'

'No.'

'Exactly.'

And I walked out and went back to class, even though I hated class. That's how angry I was.

What I wanted was a relaxed, easy conversation between two people who understood each other, where I could express what I was thinking and feeling without being judged or ordered around. I needed someone to ask questions like, 'How was it when you gave your statement to the police the other day? What happened and how did you feel about that?' Or 'So how come you and your grandparents are fighting so much at the moment?' Instead all I got was, 'You need to start trying a bit harder.'

Before the rapes I'd wanted to be a zoologist or an early childhood teacher. I was doing well at school and I was looking forward to getting into uni. After I was raped that all went out the window. The HIV medication I was taking made me feel really quiet and sleepy, which made it difficult to focus on my schoolwork. I was struggling with anxiety attacks and flashbacks. And I was so angry all the time: if someone even looked at me funny I'd blow up and then it'd be an hour, two hours, sometimes all day before I could calm down again. It was no surprise my grades were starting to slip – I didn't need the counsellor to point it out. But it took all my energy just to get through the day. I had nothing left for schoolwork.

I felt like nobody around me understood what I was going through. My body had been violated and no one understood what that was like. I really wanted someone I could talk to who understood what I was going through, someone who could help me understand all the things I was thinking and feeling, so I could start to get a better understanding of myself. Because I was starting to crack, and no one could see it.

NOT LONG AFTER THE rapes I got myself two pet mice. I kept them in a box in my cupboard. I didn't want my grandparents to know I had them, and my cat kept threatening to give me away. She was always scratching at the door trying to get at them, and if she did it while my nan was in the room I'd be surreptitiously trying to shoo her away. Sometimes Nan heard the mice moving around inside the cupboard and she'd ask, 'What is that?' I'd always play innocent and say,

'It must be Tammy scratching at the cupboard door again. I don't know what the fascination is.'

I started keeping them in my locker at school instead of at home. I carried them around with me from class to class and no one knew I had them – well, some of my friends knew. Then two of my friends got their own mice, so moving the mice around turned into this big covert operation. It didn't last of course – my friends got caught and eventually I got busted too, but I didn't get detention, and I managed to talk the school authorities out of telling my grandparents. (In fact I managed to keep it a secret from them until just before I moved out of home – I figured it was safe to tell them then, since enough time had passed that I wasn't going to get into trouble for it.) I also got to keep one of the mice – after we got busted the teacher wanted to hand it over to the science department, so we hid it in my friend's pocket. The teacher thought I'd let it go and threatened that if the school got an infestation of mice I'd have to pay for it.

The mice were cute, but the thing I really loved about them was the fact that nobody else knew I had them. They were a secret, my secret, and it felt really good to be able to keep something to myself.

# 8

# Downward spiral

THINGS WERE GOING FROM bad to worse at home. Not long before I was raped I lost my gran, and after that we lost the family home. Suddenly it seemed like all the things I counted on, everything that kept me stable, was gone.

The house I grew up in was actually my gran's house: that is, it was my nan's mum's house. My gran lived there, and so did my nan and my grandfather and me, plus Nan's sister, my auntie Geraldine, and her husband and my uncle and my cousin Paul. It was a pretty big house – it had seven bedrooms. We lived upstairs in an extension my nan and grandfather had built when my mum was a teenager. Everyone else lived downstairs.

When I first moved in with my grandparents it was like every little kid's dream had come true. I'd packed up and moved in with Nan and I was going to be spoiled for the rest of my life. I didn't have to put up with my two brothers and sister anymore. I was the only child. Every time I had a fight with my grandparents I could just go downstairs and complain to my auntie Geraldine or to my gran.

When I was little we called Nan and Gran Skinny Nan and Fat Nan. Fat Nan asked us to call her Great Nan instead, because she hated being called Fat Nan, so we started calling her Great Fat Nan, which was worse. She always said, 'But I've been on a diet!'

After my dad died, Gran became my rock. Whenever I had a problem I'd walk downstairs and have a cry and she'd listen to me and then she'd tell me stories. She used to tell me all about her childhood; how when she was a little kid she went off to live with relatives and became a scullery maid and later she became a companion to the person who raised her. Once she told me a story about how she almost got killed by a horse, and I got into trouble because I thought it was funny and I laughed. I couldn't get enough of Gran's stories. She was a nurse in the war, and she'd tell me about how a bomb hit one day and she ended up getting blown out of the bedroom window. She talked about the Germans and how at the beginning of the war they were these big burly men and by the end of the war they were just little boys asking for their mums. It was like a soap opera for me, I'd hang off every word she had to say. My gran was English and she used to complain about having to live in a sweaty, hot country. She'd moved here with her husband after the war. Gran was beautiful when she was young. She had a photo of herself when she was about twenty – she was stunning. She loved it when people told her she was beautiful, and she was always talking about how she hated old age.

As she got older my gran got dementia. She lost her short-term memory, so all she had was her long-term memory, and she started telling me the same stories over and over again. The stories I'd loved as a child started to sound like a broken record, but I still sat there and listened. There were always new things she'd remember.

As Gran got worse I moved downstairs into the room opposite hers because she needed somebody there to help her and keep an eye on her at night. Nan and I would put her on the commode and put her to bed and say the rosary with her and then I'd go to bed with my door open so I could hear her if she needed me. If Gran got up and started wandering round the kitchen at 3 am or if she lost control of her bowels and needed her sheets or her nightgown changed, Nan and I would get up and do it.

We kept her at home for as long as we could, but eventually it got to be too much for Nan, and Gran had to go into a nursing home. She was such a funny old lady. She went to one place for respite care and tried to run out of there naked. They had to put a beeper on her so she couldn't run away. She got banned from that nursing home. But then she went into permanent care, and I knew she wasn't coming out again. That was really hard, because another person I'd connected with was dying. It began to feel like every time I got really close to someone, and came to rely on them, they got sick and died.

Gran died in September 2001, when I was fourteen. Her death really upset me. Her empty room used to scare me, because even though I knew she was gone I'd sometimes feel that she was there. I used to dream about her. It was a very hard time. It was only a few months later that I was raped. And then we lost the house too.

That house had such history to it. My great-grandfather – Gran's husband, my nan's dad – had bought that house after the war and it had always been a place people came to when they needed help. Even when my nan was a little girl, there'd always been extra people staying there, people who needed looking after. As time went on they just kept extending the house so everyone who needed somewhere to live could stay there. It was a real family home, and for me it represented stability. People came and went, but the house was always there. After my dad died, and things went wrong with my mum, I knew I still had a home, because I had that house.

But when Gran died the house had to be sold. Nan's brothers and sisters had mortgages and bills to pay, and they were all in desperate need of this inheritance, so the house got auctioned off. I was furious at everybody for letting it happen. Every time the subject came up I'd yell at them all, telling them they shouldn't be forcing Nan to sell the house. They weren't forcing her – she did it willingly – but in my eyes, the rest of the family were forcing us out of the family home forever. Leaving that house just about killed me. But there was nothing I could do about it.

I was the last person to sleep in that house. Nan and Grandad had set up their bed at the new place and mine hadn't been set up yet, so I spent the last night in the old house alone. I was terrified being in there by myself: it had seven bedrooms, three lounge rooms, two kitchens, three bathrooms, about a thousand and one exits and entrances for burglars, about a thousand possible ghosts (there had been a couple of sightings). But I made it through and the next morning I felt really proud of myself.

After the house was sold, my nan and grandad moved into a new place. It was only a street away from our old house. But it just wasn't the same. The old house had been my home; the new house just felt like a place to crash. I was fighting with my grandparents a lot, and it was really beginning to feel like they didn't want me around. I suspect they felt as though they'd raised their kids, they'd done their job, and now they really ought to be enjoying their retirement, but instead they were stuck with a teenager who was in the middle of a major crisis. They were always saying that my mum ought to be looking after me, that I should be living with her. I don't think they realised how often they said it, and it really hurt, because it just made me feel like they didn't want me anymore. If I confronted them about it, they'd always say, 'Don't be silly, you have a home with us.' But it didn't feel that way to me. And what made it even more hurtful was the fact that my mum had made it really clear she didn't want me with her. I didn't actually want to move in with my mum, but I would've liked to hear her say, 'Yes Tegan, you've got a place here with us if you need it.' I would've liked to have the option. But every time I tried to talk to her about it she'd just change the subject. It felt like nobody really wanted me.

BEFORE THE RAPES I was a pretty normal teenager. I didn't get into trouble and I didn't do anything really naughty. But after I was raped, that changed. I started sneaking out at night, hanging around with bad boys, smoking, drinking, putting myself in harm's way. I knew it was risky, but I didn't care. In fact, the riskiness was part of the point. Putting myself in danger was exciting – it felt good. I told myself that bad things didn't happen twice, and since the worst thing that could happen to me had *already* happened to me, it meant I could get away with anything. At the same time, I *wanted* to get hurt; I *wanted* something bad to happen to me. Pain had started to feel good to me; inflicting pain on myself helped me to feel normal again. And after the rapes, when so much about me had become public, I wanted to have some secrets. Being bad was just another secret – and it was a lot more satisfying than keeping mice in my locker.

I know exactly when I started being naughty. It was 28 July 2002, six weeks after I was raped, and it was my birthday. I'd snuck out with my friends and I had my first real cigarette and I thought, yeah, this is great.

I'd started hanging out with some different friends: Margaret and Selina. Selina came to our school because she'd been expelled from her previous school for turning up to school drunk, and the three of us started hanging out together. What we really loved doing was sneaking out at night.

Some nights we'd stay at Margaret's house, which had really high fences and her parents used to lock the gates. We'd just wait until her parents were asleep and then we'd sneak down to the side gate (so that even if her parents woke up and heard us, they wouldn't be able to see us) and I'd boost the other girls over the gate and then climb over myself, and the three of us would run away and meet up with the guys we were spending time with and hang out with them all night. Then the next morning we'd sneak back in just before her parents woke up and pretend we were getting ourselves breakfast, when in fact we were getting ourselves dinner before going off to crash. One night I got caught on the fence while I was climbing over. I was wearing a denim skirt and it got caught on a nail sticking up. So there I was, hanging upside down on the fence while Selina and Margaret pissed themselves laughing, and then I started going off at them for laughing, and Margaret was trying to shut us both up so we wouldn't wake her parents. Most of our sneaking out was done on weekends or holidays, but we didn't see a school night as a reason not to go out. If we decided to sneak out on a school night, the next day we'd just fake sick or jig school.

Other nights we'd stay at Selina's house, and then we'd have to go out her bedroom window. It was quite high up, so we had to jump, and getting back in was quite an operation. I'd boost Selina up so she could climb in the window, but it took a bit of kicking to get up there and we were always terrified we were going to wake her parents, although we never did. Then she'd run down the hall and open the back door and let us in. It was always funny when we stayed at Selina's house – she came from quite a close-knit family and there was always a chance they were going to look in and check on her, so we used to stuff her bed with blankets and stuffed toys so it'd look like she was in it. Believe it or not, that old trick does actually work. We had a lot of close calls though. One morning Selina let me in the back door and as we were walking through the lounge room I said, 'I can't believe we just got away with that again!'

'I know, what's that, our fourth night in a row?' Selina said.

'I'm so tired, I haven't had more than a couple of hours' sleep for days – I'm getting exhausted!'

And then we heard a voice say, 'Selina, is that you?'

It was Selina's dad. He'd actually fallen asleep on the couch and he'd been right there as we were talking. Luckily for us he didn't hear what we said, but the next day he confronted Selina.

'Were you two smoking outside?' he asked.

And Selina said, 'Yes. We were smoking outside. It's a terrible habit – we're sorry. We're going to quit.'

The way we figured, that was going to cause less trouble than if she'd said, 'No, we actually snuck out to walk up to Kirrawee station, went out with a group of guys in their car when they didn't have licences, went back to their house, had a few drinks, and then we came home just before you went to work.' The guys we were hanging out with were so dodgy, but we didn't care. It was part of what made it fun.

The crazy thing is I didn't trust some of those guys as far as I could throw them. (We hung out with a few different groups of guys – some of them were guys I'd known for years, they were good for a laugh, and I knew I could trust them. But there were other guys who Selina and Margaret had met more recently, and I was never too sure about them.) When I snuck out of my own house I wouldn't let them pick me up or drop me off at home. I would walk up the road to a unit block, walk through the back and out the front to meet them so they thought that was where I lived. I always felt uneasy around them and I was never really okay about hanging out with them, but I did it anyway because I wanted to be bad. People had already changed their opinion of me over something that wasn't my fault, so I decided I'd give them a reason to change their opinion of me – it was like, 'If you thought I was a bad girl before, check *this* out!' I knew Selina and Margaret were more trustworthy than Kerry and

Sophie had ever been, but at a deeper level, I think I'd just stopped caring about myself. I was doing dangerous and self-destructive things but I didn't care.

Still, it was fun while it lasted. Eventually Selina got busted because she told the school counsellor some of what we'd been up to and the school counsellor broke the student confidentiality rules and told her parents. Selina wasn't allowed to hang out with me and Margaret after that – her parents thought we were too much of a bad influence – and then her parents moved to the city, so I didn't see her anymore. As bad as I was, I still think Selina was way more of a bad influence on me than I was on her, but her mum didn't see it that way.

I was sorry I couldn't be friends with Selina anymore, but Margaret was glad to see the back of her. I'd known Margaret longer than I'd known Selina, but Margaret had got the idea into her head that Selina was stealing me away from her, and she got all jealous and possessive. Things had come to a head just before Selina confessed all to the school counsellor. It was the night of my sixteenth birthday and we were at Woolooware train station. Margaret had put something in Selina's hair, Selina threatened to smash Margaret, Margaret pulled Selina's hair and then Selina slapped Margaret's face. I couldn't believe they were having such a petty little fight – I thought if you were going to fight, you could at least do it properly, but this was like a catfight out of *Mean Girls* or *Clueless*. I broke it up, but I couldn't stop laughing because the whole thing was so petty and ridiculous. It was the lamest fight I ever saw –

I thought it was hilarious. When Selina moved away, I think Margaret felt like she'd won the war. But it was never a war except in her own head.

After Selina left, me and Margaret started getting more and more out of control. We'd sneak out so late the trains weren't even running so we'd have to hitch rides to go and see people. Then Margaret ran away from home. She stayed with me and my grandparents for a while, but then her mother came to our house and told her she couldn't stay there anymore, so she dropped out of school and moved into the Bridge Refuge, a crisis refuge in Sutherland for young people aged sixteen to eighteen. You could only stay for three months; if you didn't break any rules you'd get sent on to an independent refuge, which was more like a home. She stayed there for ages, and the two of us started hanging out with the other kids we met there.

The refuge kids all came from broken homes, and most of them had a few problems. Some of them had been abused, some of them were on drugs, some of them had terrible histories. But I loved being with them, because I finally felt like I belonged. The refuge kids weren't like the girls I went to school with: those girls were rich and they had parents who were happily married and their lives were calm and simple and easy. They had everything they wanted and nothing ever went wrong for them. The refuge kids were poor and their parents were all divorced and there'd be some new disaster every day, because that was the way life was for them. And I felt like

I fitted right in, because after what had happened to me I was incapable of leading a normal life. Every day some new traumatic thing would happen, but the refuge kids were used to that, they'd take it in their stride and tell me it was all going to be okay. All of us had something we were trying to escape from, so we all hung out together and tried to get through it as best we could.

And one of the ways we did that was with drugs.

# 9

# So high I could forget

THIS IS HOW IT would work. One of us would get paid by Centrelink, and then that person would buy drugs, alcohol, cigarettes and Maccas for everybody else. And all their money'd be gone in a matter of days, but then someone else would get paid by Centrelink so then *they'd* shout everyone their drugs, cigarettes and food. Everyone was always shouting everyone else, so it didn't matter that most of the time you didn't have any money, because everything you needed was always covered.

By the end of Year 10 I'd pretty much stopped hanging out with anyone from my old school. I only wanted to hang out with my new friends and have a sesh (smoke weed). Year 10 finishes early – once you've done your final exams that's it for the year – and that meant I had months and months with nothing to do except get stoned. Once school was over for the year it became a daily routine: we'd go out, score some weed, chop it up, find somewhere to smoke it, get stoned, then go off and find some more so we could do the whole thing again. Or we'd buy Woodstock Bourbon and Cola and Passion Pop from the bottle shop and then go down to the oval and get smashed and play footy.

My friend Margaret drifted away and started hanging out with a different crowd, but I'd made some good friends through her among the refuge kids, and once the school holidays began I saw them every day. They were kids like Jake, who was half-Fijian and half-Australian. He was pasty white, never got a tan. He had problems at home: all he wanted was to go back to Fiji, and he stole his mum and stepfather's credit card to buy a plane ticket home, but he got busted and his parents sent him to the refuge to teach him a lesson. Jake wasn't a bad kid. He'd never done anything terrible. He wasn't violent or nasty. He'd just had bad stuff happen to him. Jake and I became very good friends.

Elizabeth was another girl I met at the refuge, and the two of us became very close. She'd run away from home, and she got in trouble with the transit police for getting on a train without a ticket. There was no way she could go back home, so she just lived in the refuge until she was old enough to move out and get a place of her own. She was one of the few kids

I knew from that crowd who never smoked weed. She just wasn't into it. And she wasn't a bad kid either. She'd just been unlucky. (I'm still friends with her today. She has a two-year-old son and lives in her own place with her boyfriend, who is also a friend of mine. In all the years I've known her, she never went home – she started her own family in order to have one.)

And then there were other kids I met, like Scott. His dad used to beat him and his mum, and eventually he got placed in foster care, but he got kicked out of his first foster home, so he went to a new foster home and got kicked out of that one, too. He got kicked out of a lot of foster homes, and he was disturbed, he was definitely disturbed. Every time you spoke to him you just picked up straight away that there was something wrong with him, and every time he took any kind of substance – alcohol or drugs – he'd get really emotional and angry and upset, and you'd have to sit there and try and talk him down again. I actually went out with him for a while, but I couldn't take it for long. He was just so emotional. It was really sad.

And then there was another guy – also an ex of mine – who used to get drunk and bash girls. I knew he was weird when I started seeing him – I didn't know he was violent. It was one of those 'learn by doing' situations. I went out with him because I thought he was hot – but that ended the night I found myself on the receiving end of his rage. He was a very unstable guy – you never knew what he was going to do next.

But a lot of the people I hung out with were basically good, nice people – who liked getting stoned.

I remember the first time I got stoned. It was a couple of months after the rapes and I was out driving around with a couple of guys. We stopped under a bridge and they pulled out a cone and started passing it around, and when it came to me I thought, oh well, why not? And so I had some too, and that was my first time. A couple of months earlier, the night of the rapes, the boys had offered me weed and I'd said no. Then I was quite shocked to be offered it, and I didn't want to have anything to do with it. But now it didn't seem so terrible, and when I smoked it for the first time suddenly it made everything seem easier.

That night when I went home Nan looked at me as I walked in the door and said, 'Are you okay? You look upset.'

'I'm just tired,' I said.

I went into the kitchen and pulled out the dinner Nan had made for me and started mindlessly eating it, and the whole time I was eating I was making up some story in my head and thinking it was funny as. My grandad came in and was trying to talk to me – I was in trouble for some reason. But I didn't care. I wasn't even trying to listen. I was in a world of my own where it didn't matter what you threw at me, I could see the funny side to everything. I went upstairs and sat in my room watching telly, and everything I watched was hilarious.

The next day I realised I'd gotten away with it: I'd come home stoned and no one had guessed. When I thought about it I realised it wasn't so surprising. My grandparents don't know anything about weed. If my dad was alive he probably would have known as soon as I walked in the door, and if I lived with my mum she might have picked up on it eventually. But I knew my grandparents would never work it out. And I was right – they never did. (I told them eventually. It came under the three-year rule: if I did something wrong and wasn't busted in three years it was safe to tell them what happened, because after three years I wasn't going to get into trouble.)

I could be having the worst day – fighting with my grandparents, flashbacks and anxiety attacks, trouble at school, bitchy remarks in the schoolyard – but if I smoked some weed, everything would be all right. I'd feel calm, I'd feel relaxed, I wouldn't have any more anxiety attacks – everything would be cruisy. And all I'd want to do was sit around with my mates and have a laugh about anything and everything, and then go off and get a massive feed. While I was stoned, you could have told me my favourite pet had been hit by a car and I wouldn't have minded. I would have just shrugged and said, 'Oh well.' Nothing was a problem, not even bulimia. While I was stoned, I could eat like a horse and feel perfectly fine. But as soon as the dope wore off, I'd go from extremely hungry to extremely full, and then I'd have to make my excuses, go away and throw up. For as long as I was stoned, nothing could touch me. I was using weed to numb my feelings so I wouldn't have to deal with them. But at the time, it was the only thing I could do. Without weed my life would have been unbearable.

I didn't spend a lot of time at home that year. At first, I was staying over at friends' houses a lot and sneaking out at night. And later, once I got to know the refuge kids, I spent a lot of nights staying at various refuges with them. There was one place Elizabeth stayed for a while which was an independent refuge, and it wasn't staffed at night. So we'd hang out there together, and at the end of the day I'd say, 'Bye, see you later,' and head out the door. And as soon as the worker left for the night Elizabeth would just let me back in again, and I'd stay without the staff realising I was there. Other nights I'd stay over at my boyfriend's place. He was 21 and a bit of a creep, but he had a place of his own, so that was cool. (It only lasted a month, maybe two. There's only so much I'll put up with for the sake of somewhere to stay. I made him break up with me in the end, which is a lot harder than it sounds.) For most of that summer I treated my grandparents' house like a crash-pad. Because that's all it felt like to me. I didn't really care where I stayed so long as I didn't have to go home.

My grandparents never found out I was a stoner, even after I started smoking at home. When my cousin Paul moved out one of the things I got from him were these huge teddy bear slippers which came halfway up my leg, more like boots than slippers. And after a while, this became my bedroom routine: I had a home-made bong I'd slip down one side of the slippers, and I had a little bowl that I'd made at school, and I'd pre-chop everything and put it in this bowl, and then slip the bowl and the lighter down the other side. Then I'd pull my pyjama pants over the top so there was no way you could see it and head downstairs to the barbecue area. My grandparents knew that I smoked and they didn't approve of it, but they kind of turned a blind eye provided I didn't actually do it in front of them. And usually they wouldn't come downstairs while I was out by the barbecue, because they thought I was having a quiet cigarette and they didn't want to disturb me – or start a fight at bedtime. So I got away with it.

The thing I loved about smoking weed at night was that it helped me sleep. After the rapes I had a lot of trouble sleeping, because of the nightmares and the anxiety attacks, but if I had a cone before bed it smoothed everything out and I'd have a really good sleep. It was like taking sleeping pills. I'd have a really calm, peaceful, mellow sleep and I'd wake up in the morning feeling very refreshed.

Whenever I compare my school photo from the start of Year 10 with my school photo from the start of Year 11, I have to laugh. In my Year 10 photo, which was taken at the beginning of the year, I've got no make-up on and I'm wearing a necklace with a cross and a friendship ring on it. I look like a normal fourteen-year-old girl. In my Year 11 photo, my hair's done up in tiny little corn-rows and I'm wearing a marijuana-leaf necklace and the blackest blackest eye make-up, and I've got a seriously pissed-off expression. No one at the school ever said anything to me about the necklace. The rules said you were allowed to wear one necklace, and I was wearing one necklace. It just happened to have a marijuana leaf on it. And maybe the teachers didn't recognise it, or maybe they just had a chuckle about the cheek of a girl who turned up to school wearing a dope necklace, but whichever it was, no one ever told me to take it off.

I spent a lot of Year 11 stoned. I'd turn up to school stoned, or one of my stoner friends would call me during class, and I'd get up and ask the teacher if I could go to the toilet and simply never come back. I don't know why I didn't get into more trouble, but no one seemed to notice I was doing a disappearing act. When I look back now, that was one of the scariest things about that time of my life: it was so easy to go off the rails, and no one seemed to realise what was going on. I was depressed, I was self-medicating, I wasn't dealing with my problems. You only had to look at me and my corn-rows and my scary eye make-up to know that things weren't right. But no one noticed.

I never got into any drugs other than weed. I tried speed a couple of times, but I just wasn't into it. The thought that I might give myself a heart attack really put me off it. I discovered I couldn't take hydro either. There are two kinds of weed, hydro and natural. Hydro is full of chemicals and it can have some really nasty side effects. I smoked it a couple of times, but then I copped some that was laced with something I was allergic to, and I went blind. The effect lasted for about an hour. I tried to get up and get myself a drink and walked into a wall. Somehow I made it to the couch, and then I couldn't get up again. Eventually Elizabeth found me. I couldn't move, I couldn't speak, and she said I'd gone completely white and I was shaking. She got me food and drinks and waited with me until the effect wore off.

But even ordinary straight-up natural weed had its downside. Once you get into the habit, you've got to smoke it every day, and if you can't get it you have cravings, which are horrible, and mood swings, which are worse, because they make you want to hurt people. It makes you really paranoid too. If you see someone whispering you think they must be whispering about you. And if you hear your friend mention they went to the beach yesterday you start building these elaborate fantasies in your head, because you said you were going to the beach and then you didn't go, and you start thinking your friend must be cranky at you for ruining their day, when in fact they were probably saying something like wasn't it a beautiful sunny day? But when you're paranoid you start to think everyone's against you and they're all talking about you behind your back. It's ironic really – one of the reasons I started smoking weed was because I couldn't handle feeling like everyone was talking about me, but smoking just made the feeling worse.

And if you want an example of how badly smoking weed can affect your judgment, here's one: I started hanging out with Sophie again. After the rapes I didn't see her for a long time. I didn't want to talk to her, I didn't want to know her. We still lived near each other, so I'd see her around – I couldn't help it. But we certainly weren't friendly. The way I saw it, she'd done nothing to help me that night or afterwards, and had chosen to side with Kerry and the boys instead of me. She wasn't somebody I wanted in my life.

But you could always rely on Sophie to get weed, even if you couldn't rely on her for much else. So for a while, the two of us started to hang around together. That was weird. Really weird. But I justified it to myself on the grounds that if the two of us were friends, it might help me win the case against the boys. Sophie had agreed to give evidence, and I thought that if we were friendly again, it might encourage her to stand up and do the right thing by me in court. We never really talked about the court case; perhaps we should have. But she told me when we started hanging around together that she believed my story about what had happened the night of the rapes and that she was coming to court, and that was good enough for me. Perhaps I should have asked her what she was actually planning to say in court, because if I'd known what kind of a witness she was going to be, I probably would have told her not to bother. But I wanted to believe she meant it.

Even at the time, though, it felt weird – me and Sophie pretending it was friendship that had brought us back together, when really it was all about the weed. Looking back on it now, I just can't believe I ever thought that was okay. But I did.

For a lot of Year 10 and most of Year 11 I smoked every day. But gradually it began to dawn on me that this wasn't what I wanted to be doing with my life. There was no dramatic turning point, no single moment when I realised I had to stop smoking weed. It was more of a gradual realisation that being a stoner wasn't actually making me happy.

It was time to take control of my life.

# 10

# Wake up

AFTER I WAS RAPED, it was hard for me to feel good about myself. One of my family once told me I was damaged goods, and that really hurt – because it felt like the truth. I felt dirty and degraded, and I started smoking weed partly so I wouldn't have to feel like that anymore. But as time went on I began to realise I *wasn't* damaged goods and I didn't have to act like I was. I was sick of feeling like shit all the time. I wanted to feel good about myself again, and I wanted other people to have a good opinion of me, too.

But my life was a mess. I had a really bad relationship with my mum – no relationship at all really – and a completely dysfunctional relationship with my grandparents. I was still going to school, but a lot of the time I was just going through the motions – I'd turn up stoned, or I'd run off halfway through the day and never come back. So school life was really a bit of a joke. And of course all my friends were stoners. I spent my days getting stoned or getting drunk in the park, hanging out with a bunch of complete idiots who people would cross the street to avoid.

The cops were always moving us on or hassling us. One day when I was out with Sophie they stopped us and searched our handbags because they thought we might have weed on us. Soph had some White Ox in her bag and the cops searched it to see if anything else was mixed in with it. (White Ox is this really bad cigarette tobacco that's mostly smoked in prison because it's so cheap.) My friends just thought it was funny, but after a while I started to find it embarrassing, knowing that people were looking at us and thinking, what a bunch of low-lifes. And that was fair enough really – we *were* a bunch of low-lifes. There were days when none of us had any money and we'd hang around the train station begging so we could get some money together to buy a stick (a stick is $20 worth of weed). That was pretty low. And there was one night when I didn't want to go home so I slept at the train station. I tried to sleep on the beach but this light kept flashing and waking me up so I slept at the station. I was beginning to feel like I should be walking around with a cardboard box, saying, 'Yes folks, this is my home.'

Hanging out with people who had a lot of issues gets to be

really draining after a while. If you have friends who break down whenever they're drunk, or go nuts and try to bash you, there comes a point where you just think, no, I don't want to be around you anymore. I can't keep doing this.

Some of my friends were beginning to come to the same conclusion. Things began happening to them that forced them to grow up, get off the weed and start getting their lives together. Margaret got pregnant. My good friend Jake found out he might have to take care of his three-year-old brother because his mum was seriously ill with cancer. (He ended up moving to Queensland. Losing him was a real blow.) My closest group of friends was breaking up and changing. Some of them began to turn their lives around; a lot of them didn't. A lot of them still haven't. I don't know how many times I've heard some idiot say, 'I run the Shire.' The place is full of druggos who think that because they spend their lives getting trashed, and are known to police, and are always threatening to bash someone over the stupidest little thing, that they're the King of the Shire. But the world doesn't end at the boundaries of the Shire, and I wanted to do more with my life than keep living inside my own little dream world.

It was beginning to dawn on me that if I let my life keep spiralling out of control, if I wasted my education and spent every day hunting for weed, if I let myself be a worthless waste of space that nobody could respect, then the boys had won. The night of the rapes, they showed me no respect at all. They treated me as if I was a worthless piece of trash. My life had fallen apart from the trauma of it. But I began to realise that I actually had a choice about how I reacted to what had happened to me. I could let myself fall apart. I could let my life be a complete disaster. Or I could pull myself together and prove that I really was a worthwhile person, a strong person, a person with values, a person you could respect. For too long, people had thought the worst of me. It was time to start setting things right.

But it wasn't just about changing what other people thought about me. I had to change the way I felt about myself. I couldn't keep getting high to stop myself from feeling things. I couldn't keep running away from the pain. I had to face what had happened to me and start finding ways to live with it.

Giving up smoking was hard, and it certainly didn't happen overnight. The first bong of the day was always the best, but that bedtime one was pretty nice too. I'd been using weed to help me sleep for a long time. I didn't know if I could sleep without it. What if I started having the anxiety attacks again? What if the nightmares started up again? But it had to be done.

I knew if I was going to have any chance of getting off weed, I was going to have to stop seeing all my old friends. Smoking and getting drunk was such an integral part of our social life I couldn't imagine hanging out with them and *not* smoking. I had friends who'd hung out with that crowd and never smoked, but I wasn't one of them and I knew I didn't have the willpower. The only way I could stop was to cut all ties with my wild life – so that was what I did.

It wasn't easy. At first I tried replacing weed with grog, hoping it would mellow me out without the side effects, but that didn't work too well. Eventually I decided I was just going to have to learn to live without it. Getting to sleep at night turned out to be one of the hardest things. For a long time I suffered from insomnia. But I found that there was an upside to stopping smoking. Once my brain started working again, I felt like I'd taken a smart pill. Weed had made me feel slow and stupid all the time, but now I found I could focus again, and it felt great.

One of the things that got me through was drama. Towards the end of Year 11 a friend of mine took me along to the Saturday afternoon drama classes they held at the Cronulla Arts Theatre, and as soon as I discovered drama I was hooked. Drama gave me something new to focus on, something to look forward to, something I could put my energy into. I don't know if I would've been able to give up weed if I hadn't found it. Drama really did change my life.

Before I started drama I had no self-confidence at all. I was shy, I was anxious about my weight and the way I looked, I was terrified I was going to do or say something stupid. I was always in agony about whether people were looking at me, worrying about what they thought of me. But drama classes make you confront those fears and get past them. Every week, we'd be asked to do stuff that'd make us look stupid, and to do it in front of other people. We had to take risks and make ourselves look like idiots and think for ourselves and be creative and trust the people around us. And I just loved it. I loved the feeling of confidence it gave me, and the feeling of freedom.

Each week we'd do different exercises, inventing different characters and bringing them to life. One week I'd be playing a rich bitch from LA, the next week my character'd be a four-year-old girl who'd just wet her pants. We had one director who was a really spiritual woman, and she asked us to create a piece inspired by a deck of cards she brought in. They were kind of like tarot cards, or crystal cards – you draw a card each day to tell you what kind of day you're going to have. They give you a goal. And we used these cards to create our characters. I had to draw three cards, and then use them to build a character. My character was someone strong, who created problems and then fixed them at the same time. I was the Liberator. The exercise was completely improvised, and we had to perform it in silence, while staying in character and doing the kinds of things our character needed to do. It was so hard! I was supposed to be creating problems and then fixing them, but I just could not cause any problems. The director had the biggest laugh watching me – she knew what I was trying to do, and she could see what I was up to, but nobody else doing the exercise with me would go along with it. They were all too busy in their own little worlds doing their own things. And their stuff all fitted together – it was only me who didn't fit. I did manage to liberate them in the end, but it took some effort.

Drama was literally a liberation for me. One of the things they taught us in classes was how to speak properly. No one had ever bothered to teach me that before, and I loved knowing that if I wanted to I could turn it on and act all prim and proper and use a lot of big words and sound like I was posh, as opposed to being from the Shire and sounding like a yobbo 24 hours a day.

It wasn't just the acting I was interested in – I loved the technical side too. I learnt how to be a sound and lighting techie and worked on loads of different productions. In the run-up to a performance I'd be in the theatre all the time – rehearsing to perform, working on the technical production, getting ready to put the show on. It was all-consuming, but I loved it.

I met a lot of interesting people there too, people I never would have come in contact with any other way. There are women there in their eighties who are still going strong – I saw one of them in there just the other day, kicking and rolling around on the floor. I met so many people who'd lived such interesting lives, I could've listened to them talk all day. There were a few people there who'd done drugs when they were younger and they'd managed to pull themselves out of it and go on to have fantastic lives. I found that really inspiring, to know that you could make a lot of mistakes, but you didn't have to be stuck with them forever – you could actually move on and do good things. I would never have guessed that some of these people had been stoners in their younger days if they hadn't told me. It was great having people like that who I could look up to and say, 'Okay, cool, you did it so maybe I can too.' I've never been good at taking advice from people if I can see they don't know where I'm coming from, but I met people through the theatre who'd lived their lives and seen a lot, and if I went to them and said, 'This happened to me today' or 'So-and-so said this to me today', they'd be able to give me a fresh perspective on things, and that really helped me.

The most inspiring thing about the people I met through the theatre was realising that you could have major issues in your life, but you didn't have to let them take over your life. These people were still managing to go to work or school, they were studying for their Higher School Certificate, they were building careers for themselves, in spite of whatever else was happening in their lives. And acting was one of the things that helped them get through.

I also had good support from a few of the teachers at my new school.

My old school only went to Year 10, so in Year 11 we all moved on to a seniors' college, which was co-ed. For the first time since primary school we were at school with boys again. I'd hoped that maybe things would be easier once I was there. We'd all be a bit older and a bit more mature. Maybe I'd finally be allowed to put the whole rape thing behind me. Of course that didn't happen. Half the kids had heard what had happened to me. The other half hadn't. Which meant I spent the next two years telling the story and listening to other people telling the story and setting people straight about the story. People were always coming up to me and saying things like, 'If you don't mind me asking, what exactly happened?' or 'So what's happening with the case?' It got to the point where I wanted to carry a tape recorder around with Tegan's Frequently Asked Questions on it, so whenever somebody asked me one of the same questions I could just play the tape instead of having to answer them.

But I didn't actually mind the people who asked me directly. At least they were interested in hearing the truth. There were plenty of other people who just wanted to use what had happened as a stick to beat me with. There was one particularly memorable fight I had with a guy in drama. I was trying to give him some constructive criticism (not an easy task because he was completely hopeless) and it turned into a fight, and one of the other people in our group said to him, 'Don't worry, she thinks she got raped, like who the hell would rape her?' When he repeated that back to me I tore strips off him. I actually made him cry. But I'm not the kind of person who's going to take something like that and not say anything. I'm going to retaliate. So I was never going to be able to fade into the background at school. Everybody knew who I was. Which meant I was always getting into fights.

And just to make it more difficult, my case was very much a live issue. I'd given my evidence to the police back in June 2002, but at the beginning there hadn't been much they could do with it. I hadn't known the address of the boys' house. I didn't even know their proper names. All I knew was that they lived in Ashfield.

I believe both Kerry and Sophie knew where the house was. They'd been back there the very next day to pick up Kerry's mobile phone. But they wouldn't corroborate my story or tell the police where to find the boys. So for a while at least, it looked like that was that. I'd spent all that time being examined and giving statements for nothing.

But then at the beginning of August my nan got a phone call from someone who'd spotted an article in the newspaper. The night of my birthday, 28 July, only about six weeks after I was raped, two more girls had been raped. One of them had made a call from a mobile phone while the ordeal was taking place, and the police had been able to use that information to track the boys down. My nan read the article and became convinced they were the same guys.

'We need to call the police and tell them,' she said.

I didn't want anything to do with it. I didn't believe it was really them, or that they'd be able to prove anything, or that it would make any difference even if they could. I just wanted the whole thing to go away. So I did nothing.

But a few days later the police called me. While they were investigating the rape of the two girls, they'd started looking at some of their other unsolved cases, making connections between them, looking at similarities between the descriptions of the houses where the rapes had taken place, the people who'd been there, and what they did. And when they compared it with my case, it matched.

The first case – the case involving the two girls – had gone to trial in September and October 2003, when I was in Year 10, and the boys' sentences were handed down in April 2004. Not long after I arrived at the seniors' college, a girl who was doing Year 12 Legal Studies told me 'We're studying your case.'

'What do you mean?' I said. My case hadn't come to trial at that point.

'The K brothers. We're studying it in Legal Studies.'

And this girl started telling me all these graphic details from the case that had gone to trial, which they'd been discussing in class.

'Stop it, I don't want to hear this!' I said. 'I know all this, I don't need to hear it from you!'

It was very weird knowing that people you saw every day were studying something that was so intimate and personal. Even though it wasn't my case, my initials were mentioned from time to time; everybody knew that TW was me, and I knew they must have been thinking, well, if this happened to those other two girls, it must have happened to her, too. Not fun.

There were some things that made it easier. The principal of the college knew what I'd been through and was sympathetic. I didn't mind talking to him about it, because I knew he'd understand. It was very disappointing for me when he left. I had a different principal in Year 12, and he seemed to have the memory of a goldfish. He'd notice that I wasn't there and then he'd say to me, 'So where have you been the last week?'

'Um, my court case.'

'Oh, what court case is that?'

'The one that's been going on for the last four years. The one where I got raped and my grandparents sent you a letter saying that I wasn't going to be here because I had to be in court.'

'Oh, okay.'

A week later I'd show up at school again, and he'd say, 'So where have you been?' I felt like putting a poster up in his office saying: 'When you walk out and see Tegan, she hasn't been wagging school, she's been at court.'

I was lucky to have a really great art teacher, Mr H, for Years 11 and 12. He was completely, totally arty-farty: he was into art and he was into drama and so the two of us got along really well, because I was completely obsessed with art too. I could blabber on about it for hours, and he was one of the few people who was happy to listen. Mr H wasn't like the other teachers. He caught me breaking the rules a couple of times, and he said he wouldn't send me to the principal if I'd clean the art room. Try to imagine what an art room owned by a male teacher looked like – I don't think it had ever been cleaned! Cleaning it was probably a worse punishment than anything the principal could have dished out. But I didn't really mind because Mr H was so good to hang out with. He treated his students as if we were interesting people with lives and minds of our own. He liked to engage with us and the work we created – he took our art seriously. He treated us like adults, and that's pretty rare at school.

Art was important to me because it gave me a way to escape. Drugs had let me escape reality and go off into a world of my own, where everything was easy and nothing was stressful. But as I began moving away from drugs I realised that instead of using drugs to escape how I was feeling, I could use my art to express my feelings. If I was angry or upset or frustrated about something, instead of smoking weed and making it go away I could get out my sketchbook and draw something. Instead of suppressing my feelings, I was actually dealing with them, and getting them out of my system in a positive way by turning them into art. Drugs let you escape reality, but art lets you control reality by giving you a way to create your own world. It can be as bizarre as you want it to be – you make up the rules. I may not have been able to control much else that was going on in my life at that time, but in my sketchbooks at least, I ruled.

Mr H was the first person to suggest I should write a book about my experiences. He'd taken an interest in my case and how I handled everything, and he told me I should try writing about it. I didn't have the first idea how I'd go about such a thing – I mean, a book's a pretty big undertaking. Where would I start? Where would I finish? What would I put in and leave out? And how long would it be? But the more he talked about it, the more I began to think, well, maybe I *could* write a book.

People often ask me how I had the strength to get through the court case and all the publicity afterwards, and there isn't a simple answer to that. But one of the things that helped me find that strength was the interest and encouragement of people like Mr H and Mrs M. They always treated me like someone who was smart and interesting and creative; and because they believed in me, it helped me believe in myself.

It takes a lot of confidence to get up in court and defend yourself. A lot of people find any kind of public speaking incredibly stressful. The idea of getting up in front of people just scares the pants off them. But thanks to my experiences with drama, and the support of people who cared about me like Mr H, when the time came for me to get up in the witness box and tell my story and deal with being cross-examined, I was able to do it. I wasn't paralysed with stage fright.

I was lucky I was able to go into court with a relatively clear head, because I was going to need every ounce of strength, confidence and intelligence I had to get through what was to come.

# 11

# Building the case

WE'D BEEN WAITING A long, long time to come to court.

I had met Detective Senior Constable Kevin Bale the day after I was raped. He was one of the police officers working that first day when I went to make my statement, and he stayed with my case right through to the end. Kevin was great to deal with because he was always ready to have a laugh with me, and I relate to humour. That first day, it was Kevin who made the crack about me having kicked one of the boys in the crown jewels. It was a relief to have something to laugh about that day – and to feel like I'd managed to get the better of one of them, even if it was only in a small way. I was never in any doubt that Kevin was on my side.

Kevin was the first member of the team who would take my case through to trial: police officers Kevin and Detective Senior Constable Tony Adams; Sheridan Goodwin, the solicitor assisting the Crown; Crown Prosecutor Ken McKay; and Rebecca Lucas, an officer from WAS (Witness Assistance Service, Office of the Department of Public Prosecutions).

In the early days things were very frustrating, because no one seemed to be in charge of my case for longer than about five minutes. If I rang up to find out what was happening, I'd be told, 'Sorry, I no longer run this case but you can call this person.' 'Sorry, I was on that case two months ago, you can call this person.' 'Wait, I lost that one a week ago, you can call this person.' 'I'm sorry but I'm not in the office right now . . .' And no one would ever call me to tell me if things were happening. But once Sheridan got the case, that all changed. She believed in keeping in regular touch. She'd call me and say, 'Hi, how're you going – just thought I'd let you know that nothing's happened. But something might happen next week, cross my fingers.' Sheridan had responsibility for all the matters involving the boys: as well as my case, there were the two girls they'd raped on my birthday, plus a fourth girl who'd been raped a month after me. Sheridan was amazing: she knew everything about the cases. Everything, every single detail. She knew my case better than I did. Sheridan was incredibly tiny, like a little mouse, and when eventually we went to court she'd turn up with all the evidence in these humongous suitcases on wheels that she pulled along. The first time I saw them my heart sank, and I thought, oh, we're in for a long haul. Those suitcases are bigger than she is!

Sheridan worked incredibly hard on all our cases, because for her it was personal. She really wanted to see all of us get justice, and she took it really hard if we didn't. Sheridan's a public servant so she gets paid squat, but she was always willing to go that extra mile if it meant she could find some new point of law or new piece of evidence that might help us convict the boys or get extra time added to their sentences. She was everything you want your lawyer to be: committed, hardworking, smart, but also approachable, supportive, with a sense of humour. I could have a whinge to her and she'd let me rattle on for hours – and sometimes she'd even join in. She worked for the courts and was a part of the system, but she had a pretty clear sense of what was wrong with it. We shared a lot of frustrations over the years.

The other member of my team was Rebecca, who worked for WAS and who was there to support me through all the court appearances. She'd ring me up from time to time while we were waiting for our court date and ask me who I was torturing in my life. Rebecca's role basically was to be my punching bag – she was the one who got to listen to me ranting about how unjust it all was, and she was also the one who had to keep reminding me to behave myself in court. She was always having to grab my foot or put her hand over my mouth or ask me if I wanted to go outside. I reckon I must have driven her crazy.

The first time I met Rebecca and Sheridan was when I was introduced to the other three girls. They'd arranged a meeting for the four of us because they thought it might help all of us feel a bit less alone. I was very interested to meet the others because I wanted to see what they were like, plus I wanted to find out how they were dealing with what had happened to them. It's not often that you get a chance to talk with other rape victims, and this seemed like a good opportunity to find out how they were coping.

So one afternoon, about six months before the first two girls went to trial, Rebecca, Sheridan and the four of us girls got together in a room to meet for the first time. One of the girls hadn't wanted to come, and had to be talked into it. The other two were happy to get together and talk. It was good to meet them, but it was a slightly awkward experience for all of us. The one thing we had in common was the fact that we'd all been raped by the same bunch of guys, but because none of us had yet gone to trial we weren't allowed to talk about the cases. We were like, 'So . . . what did you do on the weekend?' In spite of the awkwardness, I bonded with one of the other girls straight away, and we're still friends. We keep in touch from time to time. The other two, not so much. I talk to one of them occasionally, the other one I don't talk to at all. I respect the fact that they don't want to talk about it, and I don't want to bring back bad memories by ringing them up to see how they're going.

The Crown decided that they would try the cases according

to the strength of the evidence and the severity of the crimes, rather than trying them in chronological order. I was raped first, in June, but the Crown decided to try the case of the two girls who'd been raped on my birthday first, because that case was the strongest and had the charges with the highest maximum penalties. If they got a conviction, it would put most of the brothers behind bars, hopefully for a long time.

The first trial was scheduled to start in September 2003, fourteen months after the rapes had taken place. We were told my trial and the trial of the fourth victim would take place soon afterwards. I was all ready to go. My attitude was, bring it on: I knew they were guilty, they knew they were guilty, so why couldn't everybody else hurry up and come to the same realisation? I didn't know much about the court system and how it worked. I didn't care that you actually needed evidence, and that you had to prove the charges beyond reasonable doubt. I didn't get that the presumption of innocence meant the boys didn't have to prove a thing. *We* had to do all the work to prove that I really had been raped. I thought that all I had to do was tell the truth and that would be enough, everyone would take my word for it and the boys would go to jail. I quickly discovered that that's not how the legal system works.

The two girls had been raped by five boys: the three boys who raped me – Mustapha, Amir and Sabir – plus their brother Rashid, and their friend Ram. Mustapha, Rashid and Ram hired lawyers to represent them, but Amir and Sabir sacked their lawyers and decided to represent themselves. This meant that they would be able to cross-examine the victims, and when the media found out about it there was a huge scandal. Legislation was rushed into parliament to prevent accused rapists from cross-examining their victims, and it passed two weeks before the trial started. The boys would have to use a court-appointed intermediary to cross-examine the girls.

The proceedings were split into two trials, to be held back to back: Mustapha, Rashid and Ram were tried first, in September 2003; Amir and Sabir were tried in October. Both trials were big successes for the Crown: the accused were found guilty on all counts. But the trials were very hard on the girls, who'd had to give evidence twice. It was good to know the boys had been locked away (although we still didn't know how long their sentences were going to be) but it was scary to think that I still had that ahead of me. How would I cope in the witness stand? It was hard to believe that anything could be as traumatic as what I'd already been through, but what if court was even worse than school? What if the lawyers and judges turned on me and also accused me of lying?

At the end of 2003 I was finishing Year 10. It had been eighteen months now since I was raped. The other girls had got justice, but for me it was still a long way off. Originally they'd planned to try all the cases back to back, but then my case and the case of the girl who was raped a month after me (on 14 July) got delayed, and were sent to the end of the queue. My new court date was 25 October 2004. That meant I'd have to wait another whole year to even go to trial. It was immensely frustrating. I felt like I was in limbo. I was still carrying the legacy of the rapes around with me at school every day. The publicity surrounding the first trial, the changes to the law, and then the guilty verdicts, meant that the subject never seemed to go away. People kept getting reminded about it. And it never seemed to get any easier: even though the boys had been found guilty on all charges of violently raping two girls I'd never met, no one seemed to think that this might actually mean I'd been telling the truth. At school it was still the same old story: yeah, right, who'd rape her?

We'd been told the boys would be sentenced in April 2004. A week before the sentences were handed down the boys' friend, Ram, committed suicide in jail because he didn't want his family back in Nepal to know what he'd been doing. A week later, the sentences were handed down. Sabir got 22 years, with a non-parole period of sixteen and a half years. Amir got sixteen years with a non-parole period of twelve years. Mustapha, who was still only seventeen, got 22 years with a non-parole period of thirteen years. Rashid got ten years with a non-parole period of five.

I was there for the sentencing, and I didn't really know what to think about it. I was happy for the other girls, because for them the whole thing was over. They'd got justice and so they were celebrating. But for me, the sentencing was quite distressing – I knew we still had a long way to go and a lot of trials to get through, and it seemed like it was too early to be celebrating just yet. It was good to know the three boys who'd raped me were going to jail for a long time. Not long enough in my view, but then I'd be happy to see them rot in jail forever. And it was hard to be happy about Mustapha getting sixteen years. With good behaviour, he could be out by the age of 29, which wasn't a happy thought. But at least it was a start. And I was hopeful that when my case went to trial, later that year (or so I thought) we'd be able to get those sentences extended.

I soon discovered that even when the sentences have been handed down, the process isn't over. That's when the appeals start. Sabir and Amir appealed against their conviction in September 2004. The appeal was turned down. But that wasn't the end of the appealing. It was just the start.

The date for my trial had been set for 25 October 2004. I was both excited and anxious about going to court. I'd never been to court before and the whole thing was pretty scary. I had no idea what I should wear. I asked the police, and they joked, 'Don't wear anything that shows cleavage.' And then they looked at me and realised that I *had* no cleavage, so that wasn't going to be a problem for me. I tried to get a sense of what I should wear by looking at what Rebecca and Sheridan wore, since they were always in and out of court. Eventually I decided that going to court is a little bit like going to a job interview, so that's what we were aiming for.

Nan's a dressmaker, and she made me some pants to wear to court. I have my own style and I also have a weird body shape. I can't buy pants off the rack – they're either too big or too small – so I have to get Nan to adjust them or make me some. Once I had the pants, we went to K-Mart and bought tops. They became my court tops – I've still got them. Whenever girlfriends of mine have job interviews they'll say, 'Do you have any nice tops?'

'Oh yeah, I've got some court tops in there, go look.'

I spent a lot of time worrying about how I should present myself. What shoes should I wear? How should I have my hair? Should I wear make-up? Should I try to seem older than I am, mature and reliable? Or should I go in my school uniform, to remind the jury that I'm still a schoolgirl? I just had no idea. Eventually I decided to go looking neat and tidy with the make-up and the jewellery toned down, so I wouldn't look too out there.

By 25 October 2004 a year had gone by since the boys had been found guilty for the first rapes, and I'd finished Year 11. I turned up at court in my new pants, ready to give evidence, only to discover that Sabir and Amir had asked for a post-ponement on the grounds that it was Ramadan. Ramadan is the most holy month of the Islamic calendar; believers are supposed to fast, read the Koran, and think about holy things. The boys argued that the trial had to be postponed because they were weakened by hunger and that might disadvantage them in presenting their case. Sheridan and Ken argued against that, but the Crown opposed the application. The trial was postponed for two weeks – the first of many delays. In my opinion the whole thing was pretty disgraceful, because the boys seemed to be using their religion as an excuse to push the court dates back.

A few days later they asked for three separate trials, one for each defendant. It would mean the juries wouldn't be told about the whole night or the presence of the other boys, and I'd have to give evidence three times. The judge refused. Then Sabir and Amir sought another delay, because Sabir was supposedly too busy working on his appeal against the earlier conviction to prepare his defence for this one. The trial date got moved again: the new date was 28 February 2005. What a Christmas present that was.

Another year, another trial date. I was starting Year 12, and my trial was scheduled to commence just a few weeks into the school year. On the first day of the trial we went back to court to discover that Sabir had decided he wanted a lawyer after all, while Amir had sacked his lawyer and needed to find a new one. The judge rescheduled the trial again, to 16 March.

The sixteenth of March rolled around. Off we went, back to court, for the first day of the trial. Sabir had a new barrister who needed more time to study the case. Amir had sacked another solicitor and barrister. The judge gave them another week.

On 22 March, I went back to court for yet another court date. This time we had an interesting new development: Sabir's barrister had a new psychiatric report saying that Sabir was crazy and might not be fit to stand trial. I was like, 'Well, I could have told you that.' So we had to wait while new psychiatric reports were made and the lawyers did their stuff. The delays dragged on through March and into April. I was supposed to be doing trial exams at school but the endless manoeuvring from the boys and their lawyers meant I never knew from one day to the next when I'd be required in court. The Office of the Director of Public Prosecutions had to send a letter to my school asking permission for me to skip the trial exams.

In April they held a separate hearing to determine whether or not Sabir was sane enough to stand trial. The funny thing about that was he was representing himself, and all the court submissions saying that he was insane were very intelligent, very well put together, but then when you saw him in court he acted like a fruitcake, pretending he was seeing things that weren't there. He called his wife and his father to give evidence that he was schizophrenic and always had been. But two doctors said he was just pretending to be nuts, so the judge ruled the trial could go ahead.

So now we had another court date: 18 May. As I had so many times before, I got up, put on my court clothes, did my hair, did my make-up, and waited for Tony and Kevin to pick me up. They'd been absolute legends throughout the whole tedious process: every time we had to go to court, one or both of them would pick me up, they'd have a latte waiting for me, and then we'd all drive into court. Some days we'd make a game of it by taking different routes and seeing who could get there the fastest, and Kevin'd always take some short cut that took twenty minutes longer. After all the delays I thought there was a pretty good chance this was going to be just another false alarm. We'd get there and they would have sacked their barristers again, or they'd be crazy again, or there'd be some other ridiculous excuse.

But when we got there, there was no legal manoeuvring. No delays. The trial was actually on.

I was going to have to give evidence.

# 12

# Three fools

It was 18 May 2005. After all the delays and postponements it was finally happening. As I walked into the courtroom and took my place on the witness stand I was so nervous I could feel my whole body shaking. I felt like I was going to spew.

I'd waited so long for this. I was finally getting close to the moment of truth, but it didn't feel good. I just felt scared. What if I stuffed things up? What if I blew it? I imagined the judge saying, 'This girl was lying from the start so we're not even going to bother questioning her,' and then sending me home. All the stress, the anxiety, the waiting, would have been for nothing, and even worse, the boys wouldn't have been held to account for what they'd done to me. I couldn't let that happen.

The case was being heard at St James Road Court, in the centre of Sydney. It's one of the oldest courts in Sydney and has five courtrooms. Kevin and Tony told me the building was haunted – I didn't believe them, but the place does have a bit of a scary atmosphere, and the toilets (which are underground) are like a dungeon. Whenever I went down there by myself I always had ghosts in the back of my mind.

Our courtroom was tiny. The accused, their friends and family, and their lawyers sat on the left; the prosecution – my side – sat on the right. At the front of the courtroom is the judge's bench, then the witness box, then the jury box, and at the back of the courtroom is the public gallery, where the reporters and anyone else who's interested can sit. It was an open court, so anybody could come in and watch what was going on.

As I took the witness stand, the first thing I saw was the judge, Justice Hidden. He didn't look friendly, he didn't look nice, he didn't look welcoming. Sitting in front of him were a lot of other people who worked for the courts. The jury hadn't come in yet, so the jury box on my left was still empty. In front of me were the lawyers, lined up at the bar table. Sheridan was there, smiling up at me, sitting beside the Crown Prosecutor, Ken McKay, who'd be arguing the case. Next to them were the three defence barristers – later, as my frustration with the legal process grew, I nicknamed them the Three Fools. And way over on the far right was the dock, where the three boys were standing.

I hadn't seen them in years. I would have been quite happy never to see them again. Now, suddenly, there they were. Most of the time I'm pretty good at keeping my feelings under control, but occasionally everything I've been pushing down just comes up at me in a big rush, and this was one of those times. I felt a huge wave of conflicting emotions inside me. I didn't know if I should look at them or look away, if I should stand up in the box and tell them all to get fucked, if I should run off, if I should stay, if I should cry, if I should laugh . . . I didn't know what to do. It was so intense I started to shake.

Once the initial shock had passed I began to notice how much the three of them had changed. All of them had had slim, trim, muscly bodies when I met them back in 2002, but they weren't trim anymore. Prison had made them all fat. Sabir had aged a lot – he'd gotten plump in the face and he just looked gross and disgusting. Amir had lost his ponytail and was going bald. And Mustapha had gone from having the world's worst hair – when I met him it was peroxide blonde – to having short, fuzzy tufts of hair. I couldn't get over how much they'd changed in three years. I almost didn't recognise them. I hadn't thought they were attractive to start with, but now they all looked so greasy and sleazy and revolting, especially Sabir. The thought that these three guys had been on top of me, that they'd actually been inside me, made me want to spew. I actually gagged – that's how disgusting it was.

I wasn't sure whether I should be looking at them or not,

but then Mustapha looked straight at me and began shaking his head at me, as if he was implying that I was a terrible liar, and that made me so angry it chased all the other emotions away. So I didn't vomit or cry or panic or freak out. I got mad. And that made me feel strong again.

Justice Hidden started to explain what the procedure would be.

'This is not meant to be an *ordeal* for you,' he said. 'If at any stage you want a break because you're feeling a bit upset or you're feeling tired . . . if you need a break, just let me know. That won't be a problem.'

It was time for the jury to come in. Justice Hidden sent me outside while the jury were brought in, and when I came back in and sat down in the witness box again the jury were there waiting for me. There were eight women and four men on the jury, and they looked friendly enough. I had to wonder if they were going to understand me and what I'd been through, since none of them looked anything like me. But they appeared to be a reasonable enough bunch.

Ken opened the questioning, asking me a lot of fairly straightforward questions to remind the jury about who I was, where I was, and how I got to be there. Then came our most important piece of evidence: the videotaped statement I'd made nearly three years earlier. This was the statement I'd started making the morning after I was raped and then finished two days later, when it was all still very recent and very fresh. I didn't really want to sit in court while the tape was being played, so I was allowed to go upstairs to the CTV room and watch it from there. It was weird enough watching a fourteen-year-old me talking about rape, let alone watching it along with 100 people I've never met before, not to mention the people I hate the most – the boys who raped me. The CTV room had a couch and table in it; it was a much more comfortable space to sit and wait than anywhere else in the building. Kevin and Tony used to bring their laptops and work in there whenever they had a chance; we ate our lunch in there as well. I spent about three days there at the start of the trial, waiting to get in the witness box.

It was strange watching my fourteen-year-old self giving evidence, because I really looked like a little girl. I looked tiny. Not tiny thin, but I looked like a young kid: I had a bad fringe that I'd pulled down and bobby-pinned, and a big ponytail on top of my head, and really bad make-up, and bad clothes my nan had picked out. It was obvious how shy I was, because I had my head down and I was playing with my hands the whole time. I wasn't that girl anymore. I'd grown up a lot in three years. The Tegan the jury saw in court was much stronger, much thinner, and a whole lot more confident than the Tegan the boys had met. And that's why the videotape was such good evidence. You could see from the tape how young and how vulnerable I'd been, you could see how upset and traumatised I was, and most importantly, everything was still horribly fresh and clear in my mind. Three years later there were little details I wouldn't have remembered without the video evidence to jog my memory. And of course having the tape there meant that I didn't have to go through the stress and trauma of retelling everything. They just played the tape, and then I was cross-examined, which made it a little bit easier. I still had to go over and over everything, but I only had to do it fifty times instead of a hundred times.

When the tape had finished, Ken asked me to clarify a few details, like, 'Where were you examined? Was that at the Children's Hospital at Randwick?'

'Yes.'

That part was easy.

But then the first barrister got up. His name was Adam Morison and he was appearing for Sabir. He had this disbelieving look on his face, and I quickly came to loathe him. His one mission in life seemed to be to make me look like a liar. He picked on little things, like the fact that I told my nan I was going to a Nutrimetics party when I wasn't. Any sensible person could see that that was just a normal teenager telling their parents a lie so they could go out somewhere, but he made it out to be one lie in a chain of lies that showed I was a massive liar who lied about everything. Every question he asked was intended to trip me up, as if by constantly picking at little tiny inconsequential details he could somehow make my entire story unravel. But when you're telling the truth it's hard to trip up.

While the questioning was going on I kept looking out into the courtroom to try and get a sense of how it was all going, hoping that someone out there would smile back at me. It's a pretty uncomfortable feeling, sitting in a witness box in front of a court full of people, including the three guys who raped you, and it can be hard to know where to look. Sheridan would always give me a smile if she didn't have her head buried in a heap of legal books, trying to find some law to slam the boys with. I looked at the jury a few times, but whenever I did I just wanted to scream at them, 'These guys are a bunch of liars. They've raped other girls and you're not allowed to know.' So I didn't really want to look at them. And occasionally I looked over at the boys, but that was a big mistake. Whenever I looked at them I'd see them smirking back at me, or mouthing how much they hated me, telling me to get fucked. They looked so evil sitting there. So I tried not to look too often in their direction.

Morison questioned me all day. He used a lot of big words, maybe because he thought I wouldn't understand them, but I'm a fairly articulate person with a large vocabulary, and I don't mind using big words myself. I had no trouble understanding his questions and answering them. But then he'd just ask me the same question again in a slightly different way, until I was about ready to scream with frustration.

Of course, most of them didn't even seem to be relevant questions at all. He never asked anything like, 'Did the boys have a knife to your throat or did they just threaten you with a knife?' Oh no. He asked things like, 'Was the light on or was the light off?' Or 'Did they kiss you on both cheeks or just one when you greeted hello?' He was hoping that if he could catch me out by getting some little tiny detail wrong – like whether I'd been kissed on both cheeks or just one cheek, or whether it was the right cheek first or the left cheek, that somehow that would discredit my entire story. I couldn't understand why he kept going on the cheek-kissing thing, but then when Soph got up and gave her evidence I discovered she'd told the police the cheek-kissing thing never happened.

And he kept trying to insinuate things that weren't true. He asked me about the car journey to the boys' house.

'Would it be fair to say that you, when you were in the car and coming into the house, that you were a bit quiet?'

Of course I was bloody quiet! I didn't know who I was with.

'Is that because you were, at that stage, a bit shy? Nervous about the evening?' He was trying to imply that I was 'nervous and shy' because I'd gone there intending to have sex with the boys, which was totally untrue.

And he kept asking me if there were lights in the house.

'See, I suggest to you, Tegan, that there were no lights on in the lounge room at all during the course of the evening . . .'

He must have asked me about the lights twenty times. I said to him, 'There *were* lights on in the lounge room. There is a difference between light and dark . . . I can *tell*.'

The longer it went on, the more angry and fired up I got. I was furious with Morison for the way he was treating me. And whenever I caught a glimpse of the boys I'd just want to take to them with a crowbar. The longer I stood there in the witness box, the more I felt like it was *me* who was on trial.

Finally, we took a break. It was only a short recess but I got to go outside and have a bit of time away from Morison. My team kept telling me I was doing really, really well and trying to encourage me to keep going, but it didn't feel like I was doing well. Morison made me feel like a little piece of dirt who'd decided to tell a whole lot of lies about a nice bunch of boys because I was such an evil, lying, filthy little slut. It felt like the defence could say whatever they liked about me, and I couldn't do anything to hit back or even show how I felt, because it might harm my chances. I had to be sweet and nice and good and patient while the defence barristers made me out to be something I'm not, but the jury weren't even allowed to know something that had already been proven in court: that these boys are convicted rapists. I just couldn't get over how unfair it all was.

When we went back in and the questioning started again, Morison started asking me about the drinks, which had been put on the coffee table in the middle of the lounge room, not far from the sofas.

'And anyone that was sitting there could easily reach over, pick up the glass, or pick up a bottle of vodka, Coca Cola if they wished to? Would you agree with that, it was accessible?' he asked me.

He tried to imply that I was pouring vodka for myself, as if I was a teenage alcoholic. In fact I was a dumb, naïve and trusting teenager: the boys gave me drinks, and I drank them. I was stupid, yes. A hardened drinker, no.

Morison started turning into a real bastard after that. 'The alcohol was starting to take effect and you were feeling good, weren't you?'

'No. I wasn't.' But, I mean, who cares if I was?

'No one was telling you to keep on drinking, were they?'

'They were pouring more glasses and putting them in my hands. That's pretty much the same thing.'

'Seeking to blame others for your own actions, weren't you, Miss Wagner?'

'I'm not blaming anyone for anything.'

I couldn't believe he said that. A bunch of older boys took three fourteen-year-old girls into the middle of nowhere and got them all drunk and then raped one of them and *I'm* the one seeking to blame others for my own actions? I could feel the anger swelling up inside me. The stress was making my psoriasis break out in red, angry blotches all over my body and I could feel them getting hotter and darker.

But instead of breaking down, I turned to look at the boys just to see if they could feel my telepathic waves of hatred. I just wanted them to know how much I despised them. I wasn't going to let them get to me. I wasn't going to cry in front of them. I was going to win.

But first I had to get through Morison's questioning.

He started asking me more questions, like, 'Were you attracted to anyone? Was anyone attracted to you? You were

attracted to this particular person, weren't you, Miss Wagner?'
For starters, my name is 'Tegan', not 'Miss Wagner'. I hated
getting called Miss Wagner. That's my mother and my grandmother. And as I've said before, at the time of the rapes I
thought I looked like a baby hippo so I certainly didn't think
anybody was attracted to me. And I definitely wasn't attracted
to them. Before I even knew anything about them, I thought
they were rude, smelly, scary and untrustworthy. So no,
I wasn't attracted to them.

At one point Morison stumbled with one of his questions
when he asked me what I did after I'd gone to the bathroom.
My recollection of the night is that I went to the bathroom
twice before I was raped. That is how I've always remembered
it. That's what was in my statement and that was what I said
in court. But Morison had forgotten that.

Eventually I said, 'I left the lounge room twice to go to the
bathroom. Which time are you talking about? The first or
the second time?'

He said, 'I thought I'd made it clear. I'm talking about when
you got up. There were two boys either side of you, as I understand it.'

I couldn't help but chuckle as I watched him make a fool
of himself. I just looked at him with a small grin and went,
'Mmm.' He'd avoided my question and he knew it. It was a
little moment of revenge.

Things went downhill when we went back after lunch.
Morison kept hammering me over details, asking the same

questions endlessly. I felt like I was going to cry but I didn't want to cry in front of the boys. I'd been on the witness stand for a full day now and he'd just been repeating the same questions over and over and over and over again. The rapes themselves didn't take that long.

Then Morison started suggesting I had initiated everything. My recollection of the night is that Sabir put his arm around me, and I didn't feel comfortable with it. But Morison was suggesting that I made the first move.

'You put your right hand on his left thigh and began to stroke him?'

I nearly died. I would never have dreamed of doing something like that when I was fourteen. I said, 'That was so far incorrect!'

'He placed his left arm around your shoulders?'

'I never put my hand on him, I never stroked his leg, I never touched his leg. I sat there with his arm around me.'

Morison started saying that I was flirting with Sabir because I'd been drinking. He suggested that I'd known Sabir was hitting on me, and I'd let him put his arm around my shoulders because I wanted him. He tried to make me sound like a promiscuous little slut. He kept harping on this idea that I was drinking voluntarily. He tried to suggest that when I was first in the bedroom I'd asked for a drink – an alcoholic drink – when in reality I'd been asking for a coffee because I was desperate to sober up. He also kept trying to confuse me about which boy had been in the room first, suggesting it had been

Sabir when I knew it was Amir. Eventually I told him, 'I never got any sort of beverage when I was in that room and if you'd read my statement carefully, sir, you would know that it was Amir, not Sabir.'

Morison then suggested that regardless of who the person was – whether it was Sabir or Amir – he put it to me that I left the room after five minutes or so of kissing this person to go get another vodka.

'Sir, the only time I left the bedroom was when the light was turned on and I ran out of it. That's the only time. I was in that bedroom for the whole time so don't suggest otherwise.'

But Morison made out like I was happy and smiling. He said I'd said, 'He's waiting for me in the bedroom.' He suggested that I knew what was going to happen and that I was completely fine about it.

'If you don't mind me saying,' I said, 'that's complete bullshit!'

If I'd had a conversation with the girls, the first thing I would have said was, 'Please can we go. I don't like this!'

It just went on and on, with Morison suggesting I'd brought the condom Mustapha had used, that I'd told the boys I was fifteen instead of fourteen because I was there to have sex with them, that I fondled Sabir, that I undressed him and let him undress me, that I'd said 'I want to do it 69-style,' and that when Sabir refused – if you can believe that – I'd asked if I could suck his dick.

By this stage I didn't know what to do. I was feeling hot

and shaky and I wanted to yell at Morison, or cry. The stress was so intense I'd simply shut down. I was still standing in the witness box, I was still answering questions, but I have no recollection of what was said to me or what I said in reply. (I've had to look at the court transcripts in order to write this chapter.) I just couldn't believe the boys would have the nerve to suggest that it was me who'd been saying all these sexual things when it was them who were forcing unwanted sexual acts upon me. All I could say in response was, 'That never happened. No, that did not happen. No, that did not happen.'

It was just so degrading. The story Morison told about that night made me out to be nothing but a common slut – as if the boys had been paying me in alcohol to do stuff with them. In Morison's version of the story, after I'd finished having consensual sex with Sabir I asked him, 'Did you come inside of me?' And he said, 'No, I had the condom on.' (The condom which, according to him, I'd brought.) Then he took the condom off and said, 'I'm sorry, it seems it has broken . . .' at which point I went from being passionate and willing, to crying hysterically. 'My God, I could get pregnant!' That is so far from the truth it's not funny, but that's what Morison told the court. He asked me if I remembered all this.

'No. Because it never happened. The whole thing's fantasy.'

I couldn't take it anymore. I felt the hot tears welling up

in the back of my eyes and that real lump in your throat when you want to start crying. I knew I was about to lose the plot, and I had to get out of there. I turned to the judge and said, 'I'm sorry, can I please have a break?'

I ran out of the courtroom and Sheridan and Rebecca came after me. They stood there and talked to me for a bit, trying to get me to calm down. Sheridan told me she could see how stressed I was on the stand because I just looked purple. She said she'd been worried I was going to crack. She wasn't the only one – I felt like I was ready to crack. The only reason I was holding it together was because I didn't want the boys to see me buckle. But I didn't know if I could handle any more of this, and I still had two barristers to go.

Fortunately I didn't have to go back into the witness stand that day. The judge decided to call it quits, so I wouldn't have to face Morison and the boys again until the following day.

The judge had told me it wasn't supposed to be an ordeal. Looking back, it sounds like a bad joke. Lawyers aren't supposed to harass witnesses, but it seemed to me that the lawyers for the defence were there to tear me apart. How could that not be an ordeal?

That night I wasn't allowed to talk to anyone about what had happened. I couldn't talk to my family, I couldn't talk to my friends. I wasn't allowed to discuss my statement or my evidence with anyone until I'd finished being cross-examined. It was very hard not being able to debrief about the day. My whole world revolves around being able to talk to my friends. If I could talk to my friends, then I could vent. And if I could vent I could get over anything. Instead, all I could do was stew.

But even if I *had* been able to talk to my friends, I don't know if they really would have got it. I don't think anyone could have imagined just how hard it was to have to stand there in court with lots of people staring at me, while a lot of smart, aggressive, highly paid people did their best to blacken my name and demolish me. And I wasn't allowed to fight back. I had to just suck it all up. No amount of drama classes can prepare you for the reality of a rape trial when you're the victim. By the time I got home that night I wasn't sure what I was going to do the next day. I didn't want to have to get up and do it all again. I didn't want to go back to court. I didn't want to hear what lies the other two boys had told about me. I just wanted to sit in my room for the rest of my life and never leave.

But when I woke up the next morning I was ready to take the fight back up to them. I reminded myself that these guys had already been convicted once. In a way, I'd already won, and all the lies they were telling about me were just their way of getting back at me. They were trying to have one last little go at me, as if they hadn't done enough already. But I wasn't going to let them intimidate me.

The second day began with a bit of legal argument. After that was over I went back into court. I wasn't as nervous and I found I was more willing to confront the boys than I had been yesterday. Today I could look at them, I could stare down at them and I had no problem with them whatsoever. Yesterday they'd seen me go through hell and I came out still standing. I knew nothing could be as bad as yesterday so I just kept staring at them and letting them know what I thought of them. Every so often they'd stare at me and shake their heads and I'd just look back at them and smile.

Morison went on and on and on with his questions that he repeated a thousand times in ten hundred different ways, repeating Sabir's gross and disgusting version of events. I just took the whole thing in my stride and refused to let him get to me. According to the court transcripts, Morison asked me 856 questions. At last he finished his cross-examination and we took a short break.

I felt so much better knowing I'd just stood up to him in front of the three people I will always hate. Morison had asked me the foulest questions and I'd been able to stand up to him. Knowing I'd made it through gave me a real sense of strength and accomplishment. Morison may have been loathsome, but what he didn't realise was that by actually pressing Sabir's version of events and putting those questions to me, he made it easier for me to stand up and tell the truth. Because if you *know* the truth, if you *know* what really happened, it's easy to stand up to someone, no matter how much they bully and harass you.

He kind of made me laugh towards the end. Even after he'd finished cross-examining me I felt like he was still trying to intimidate me just by looking at me. He'd sit there at the bar table giving me this stupid look while the other barristers were questioning me. I wished I'd had a mirror, because if he'd seen what he really looked like he never would have done it again.

After Morison, the rest of the cross-examination was easy. I was still asked a lot of stupid questions, but the other barristers weren't as unpleasant as Morison, and Amir and Mustapha's version of events weren't as revolting. Amir made things up, just like his brother, and pretended he was Mr Innocent, but he didn't invent anything too degrading, like saying I asked for it 69-style.

By the time I'd finished with Amir's cross-examination I felt *so* much better. I knew that I still had a long way to go and I knew that we still had to get a verdict, but I felt like the jury were finally starting to believe me. Most people think that when something bad happens to you, you should be upset and crying. At the beginning I was worried that because I wasn't an emotional wreck the jury might not believe I was telling the truth. But by the end of it I trusted them to have worked out that I wasn't the crying type – I was a strong girl who was standing up for herself, who wasn't lying, and who was just defending herself in a court of law.

Morison had cross-examined me for nearly two days; Amir's barrister cross-examined me for a day. Mustapha's barrister cross-examined me for less than half a day. He never really gave me a chance to tell my version of what happened. Mustapha's story was that he wasn't there and that he only went into the room where I was raped to get some money for a bet. Whether or not he went into the room to get money for a bet is irrelevant; he still raped me while he was in there. He said he didn't, and because he used a condom there was no DNA evidence. So it was my word against his.

By the time Mustapha's barrister had finished cross-examining me I felt great. The ordeal was finally over and I was the happiest girl in the world. I was so ecstatic, I felt like doing cartwheels. It was finished. I'd come to court wanting to make the boys feel powerless, to make them feel that no matter what they tried, or what they threw at me, I was always going to be around and I was never going to let them get away with it. I was the reason they were in court, and I was the reason they were going to be made to pay for what they'd done. They'd made me feel powerless, but now I had the power, and I'd used it to bring the full weight of the law down on their heads. And I was just so proud of the fact that I'd actually done it. I'd got up there, and I hadn't cried or faltered, I'd given evidence as well as I knew how. Three years ago they'd picked on me because they thought I was weak, but they were wrong. I'd shown them just how strong I really was. I wanted them to look back on this and think, *oh my God, we really did the wrong girl*. Because they really really had.

I knew we weren't out of the woods yet. We still had to wait for Kerry and Sophie's evidence and we still had to sit around and listen to all the other stuff – police statements, hospital reports, all that stuff. But my part was over.

# 13

# The rest of the trial

I WATCHED THE REST of the trial from the public gallery. Some days I turned up in my school uniform, looking a bit more like my normal self: heaps of jewellery, heaps of make-up, pull-up stockings falling down around my ankles, a uniform that was too big for me because I'd lost so much weight, my blazer tied around my waist. Tony and Kevin were laughing at me because I'd looked so respectable while I was giving evidence and now I looked – well, not so respectable. But it didn't stop Amir's lawyer from objecting to me being there because I might influence the jury by sitting there in my uniform. They'd already seen me giving evidence as a fourteen-year-old so I didn't see what difference it could possibly make. Neither did the judge. He let me stay.

The rest of the trial was a bit like a soap opera, with witnesses lying on the stand and the boys changing lawyers all the time and doing their best to abort the trial. The delays and frustrations continued. I'd go to court and they'd tell me, 'Yeah, we're probably not going to start for a couple of hours.' Oh, why not? 'Sabir fired someone.' Oh. 'Amir fired someone.' Oh, okay, all right. 'They both fired someone.' Okay. 'Oh, they're thinking about firing –' Until I wanted to say to them, just keep the freaking barrister! You're not going to win the case anyway!

Those boys completely exploited Legal Aid. Legal Aid needs to be fixed. They were constantly hiring and firing lawyers, all at taxpayers' expense, solely so they could try and delay the trial. They were hoping that one of two things would happen: either they'd manage to delay the trial long enough so I'd no longer be a minor and my videotaped evidence could no longer be used; or they'd wear me down enough that I'd decide it was all too hard, and the trial would be abandoned. My eighteenth birthday was on 28 July; the clock was ticking. But there was nothing anyone could do to stop them and their stupid games. Legal Aid threatened a couple of times to stop providing them with lawyers, but then they gave them lawyers anyway. It was a joke.

Kerry was called to give evidence. It seemed to me that she had one goal on the witness stand: to protect Mustapha. She didn't seem to care if she dropped Amir and Sabir in it, so long as she protected him. I think she had a crush on Mustapha, and maybe that's what motivated her. Kerry's story was that Mustapha was in the lounge room with her the whole time, and only left the lounge room for maybe two minutes. On the stand she said she never heard any noises coming from the room where I was raped, and that she had no idea that anything was wrong with me until I came out of the bathroom crying.

It was so frustrating for both me and the Crown listening to her give evidence. She'd made two statements to the police, one on 16 June 2002 (the Sunday after I got raped) and then another in October 2004, when the case was being prepared. The two statements were contradictory, and in the second one she admitted that she'd lied in the first one. The problem for us was that we couldn't get either of her actual statements entered as evidence. The only evidence we could present was what she was willing to say on the witness stand, and that was almost nothing. In her statement, she'd said that Mustapha had told her I'd kicked him and that he'd hit me, and he'd shown her the room where I was raped and she'd seen the condom on the floor. She said she'd heard noises coming from the room too. But when she got up in the stand, she wouldn't repeat any of it. Ken did his best to get around this problem by reading out parts of her statement and asking her if she recalled any of it, but she claimed to have forgotten just about everything. The defence lawyers did the same thing, reading out some of the things she'd said in her first statement, when she was desperate to make it look like the whole thing was my fault and that neither she nor Mustapha had done anything wrong. They read out the parts where Kerry claimed that I was flirtatious, that I was all over Sabir, that I was pouring my own drinks, that I willingly went off to the bedroom with one of the boys, that I'd gone there planning to spend the night. (The most ridiculous thing she said was that it was Sophie who'd stolen my undies from my bag and thrown them in the bin, not her. Why would Sophie do that? She'd only just met the boys; why would she take my undies to protect them?) Kerry claimed she didn't remember much of that either, but even so it was pretty damaging.

I was sitting in the public gallery while she was on the stand, and every time they read out one of her lies I wanted to get up and shout at the jury, 'She's a liar! Don't listen to her!' But I couldn't. I wasn't allowed to show any emotion or argue or do any of the things I was desperate to do. Every single time she said something I didn't like, I'd have Rebecca sitting there next to me trying to calm me down, saying, 'Tegan, Tegan! No, don't shake your head, don't shake your head! You're not allowed to say anything. It's okay. It's all right.' I really just wanted to get up and abuse the crap out of her, but I knew that if I did that the whole case would have to be restarted and I would've had to go through everything all over again. So I had to just suck it up. But it was really hard. I couldn't understand how a girl who had been such a close friend of mine could do such a thing to me.

I knew I shouldn't have expected anything from Kerry. I didn't really think she was going to turn around and corroborate my story in court. After everything she'd done, of course she was going to take that attitude. I just kind of hoped that her conscience would get to her and she'd decide to tell the truth for my sake. But she didn't. She was only interested in protecting Mustapha, and she didn't care what she said about me. By the end of it, I hated her just as much as I hated the boys.

Sophie was a different story. Kerry had taken sides long ago, but Sophie still thought she could give evidence in court without siding with anyone. For her, it was a question of whether to take my side, or Kerry's side – she wasn't so concerned about the boys. It didn't matter to her whether they got locked up or whether they stayed out and raped other girls. For her, the real question was, would she do the right thing by taking my side, or would she make life easier for herself by taking Kerry's side? Sophie and Kerry were still hanging out in the same sort of world – weed, dodgy people – and they still occasionally crossed paths. Sophie might have believed that if she took my side there would be repercussions, and must have feared for her own safety. After all, Kerry had told us both that if the boys found out we had gone to the cops they would kill us all.

Then, of course, there was the problem with the statements.

Like Kerry, Sophie had given two statements to the police, one right after it happened, the other in October 2004. And also like Kerry, Sophie had told quite a lot of lies in her statements, especially the first one. If she confessed that now, there was a chance she could get in trouble with the police.

It took a bit of effort to get Sophie into court in the first place – she was ordered to appear so she could give evidence but in typical Sophie fashion she just failed to turn up, switched off her phone, didn't return calls, wouldn't answer messages. The police went around to her house and warned her to be in court the next day or there'd be trouble. Did she show? No. After a couple of days of no-shows the judge issued a warrant for her arrest. That seemed to frighten her into toeing the line, because she did finally appear in court.

Once she got up on the stand, it turned out her memory loss was even worse than Kerry's. The lawyers would ask her a question. She'd say she couldn't remember. They'd give her a copy of her statement to look at, and then ask if that helped refresh her memory. 'Not really,' she'd say. Just as they had with Kerry, the lawyers were reduced to cherry-picking bits from her statement and asking her to read them out, while she claimed she had no memory of events. I don't know what she thought she was doing, but she only succeeded in muddying the waters, making it harder for us to get a conviction.

I spoke to her afterwards, outside court, once she'd finished giving evidence. She couldn't understand why I was upset with her.

I said to her, 'Sophie, you didn't defend me at all. You agreed with everything that was put to you.'

All she said was, 'It's been so long that I don't remember everything.'

There's not much you can say to that, is there? So I just said, 'Thanks for rocking up.'

But really, I wanted to kill her. I wanted to kill both of them, Kerry and Soph, for lying to the police and then standing up and lying again in court. Listening to them give evidence was one of the hardest parts of the whole trial, because I had to sit there and listen while they lied about my case, but I couldn't show any emotion or argue back. I made Rebecca's life hell on the days when Kerry and Sophie were giving evidence. When I get tense my foot starts to jiggle, and my foot was jiggling so much she had to grab it constantly. I couldn't stop myself. It was either jiggle or explode.

My nan and my auntie were also put on the stand, although it was only for a few minutes each. They were asked stupid questions. My auntie was asked, 'Did Tegan really call you on the morning of the fifteenth of June to tell you she was raped?'

'Yes.'

'Okay, thank you. That's it.'

It was literally one or two questions. My auntie had to fly all the way down from Ballina to give evidence. At least she didn't have to pay for it, and she got to visit the family while she was in Sydney. But it seemed a bit pointless to me.

In between listening to the evidence I spent a lot of time trying to work out what the jury were thinking. Obviously I wasn't allowed to talk to them, and they weren't allowed to talk to me, but I could watch them and try to guess how they were responding to everything that went on. Every so often I'd see one of them jot something down and I'd start racking my brains about how I'd acted, how I'd behaved, wondering if they were thinking that I was this little snot-nosed brat that just deserved everything she got. But there were at least a couple of people on the jury I felt I could connect with. There was one girl who looked like she wasn't much older than me, and I kept hoping that she was hearing this and sympathising. There were a couple of guys on the jury, but they didn't look like the sort of people who'd sympathise with the boys. They looked like the kind of guys who would want to listen and hear the rest of the story. There were another couple of women who actually looked a little bit scary, and I thought if I was going to get a guilty verdict, they'd be the reason we got it. Every so often you could see how angry they were, although they weren't supposed to show their emotions. You could tell by the way they reacted – taking notes about things that were said, turning around to see who was in court that day. They were taking everything in and working out for themselves what was going on, and gradually I began to feel like they were on my side. Every time I looked up I'd get a little bit of a smile, or a friendly look that gave me hope. And that gave me the confidence to keep going.

All up, the trial took nineteen days. I wasn't there for all of it because I was trying to catch up on the school I'd missed. The days I missed turned out to be some of the most exciting, because Sabir was doing his best to abort the trial. He sacked yet another barrister, and then Legal Aid announced they wouldn't provide him with another one (they changed their mind later). He sent a note to the judge telling him he was insane and needed psychiatric assessment. The judge refused to have him assessed. Then, on the thirteenth day of the trial, Sabir jumped up and told the jury that he and his brothers were convicted gang-rapists and that they were already doing 22 years for raping other girls. He thought if he did that there was no way the trial would be allowed to continue and that we'd have to start the whole process *again*.

I could have shot him. I couldn't believe he'd done it. I mean, I would have loved for the jury to know everything the boys had done to those other girls, but I understand why the system is the way it is. The jury was there to make a decision about the facts in my particular case; just because other girls were raped by these guys, it doesn't necessarily follow that I was. The jury shouldn't have their opinion influenced by other events that weren't directly part of this case. It's only fair that the boys should get tried for this crime, and that it should be a fair trial. But when someone like Sabir chooses to deliberately tell the jury things they shouldn't know in an attempt to abort the trial, that isn't fair.

He only partially succeeded. Justice Hidden decided to

abort Amir and Mustapha's trial, but as far as Sabir went, the Crown argued that it was his own stupid fault the jury had heard something extremely prejudicial and so his trial should be allowed to continue.

I was desperate for it to continue, and not just because I didn't want to go through cross-examination again. After everything Morison had put me through, I really wanted to hurt Sabir. I wanted to get him, and I was positive that with all the stunts he'd pulled, and with my cross-examination and everything else that had been said, I was going to get a guilty verdict. After everything he'd done, we couldn't let him start the whole process again with a new jury. Luckily for us, Justice Hidden agreed with the Crown. So Sabir's trial continued with the same jury.

Sabir was furious that his trial hadn't been aborted and he kept doing whatever he could to disrupt it. One day he smuggled pears into court, hidden in his pockets, and threw them at the jury. (He missed.) The judge told the jury they had to remain impartial and not let that incident affect their decision. I thought it was wonderful – how could it not affect their decision, when they saw what a horrible, violent creep he was?

The rest of the case was spent with him in and out of shackles – he was put in them because of his threatening behaviour, but then the judge would rule that it was prejudicial for the jury to see him in shackles, so they'd be taken off again. Then he'd do something else threatening and they'd be put back on again. One day he jumped the dock and threw a water glass at the mothers of two of the other victims, who were sitting in the public gallery. He missed again, but it scared the absolute daylights out of them. Then he grabbed the water carafe off the table and smashed the end of it and started threatening people. Sheridan had to jump under the table and it took two officers of the court to get him back under control.

The last evidence given in the case was Sabir's own. He got up and told his version of the story, the version Morison had put to me: that I was flirting with him, that I wanted him, all that degrading stuff about me asking him for 69 and offering to suck his dick. Ken cross-examined him for a full day, picking all the holes in his story. Sabir gave quite a performance in the witness box. As he was cross-examined he started crying and sniffling – not to show contrition, of course, because he was sticking to his story that the whole thing was consensual. No, he was crying because he wanted to convince the jury that the whole case against him was a complete fabrication and he was totally innocent. This was the last thing he said in the witness box, with tears rolling down his cheeks: 'I explained to you what was the truth. I did not come to this country to rape woman. I immigrated to this country for a better future.'

Kevin and Tony couldn't believe it. They thought he was just a gutless wonder. I couldn't believe Sabir thought anyone on the jury could possibly feel sorry for him after all the evidence they'd heard and everything he'd done during the trial. But that was Sabir – he still didn't think he'd done anything wrong and he thought he could make the rest of the world go along with his version of events.

But at last, after nineteen days of trial, and nearly three years of waiting, the evidence was finished. The lawyers made their closing statements. And then the jury was sent away to consider their verdict.

The ordeal was almost over.

# 14

# The verdict

WAITING FOR THE JURY to come back with a verdict was probably the most nerve-racking part of the whole experience. The case was closed, we'd said everything we could possibly say. If there was anything important that we'd left out, or some lie the boys had said that we hadn't managed to correct, it was too late to do anything about it now. The whole thing was out of our hands. There was nothing more we could do, except wait.

I just didn't know what to expect. To me, the evidence had sounded pretty damn convincing, but I didn't know if the jury felt the same way. What if they believed the boys' stories? What if they didn't realise they'd been lied to by some of the witnesses? I didn't know what I was going to do if the jury came back with a verdict of not guilty, but I had to consider the possibility that they would. My worst fear was that the jury would turn out to be just like all those people at school who'd said, 'Who'd want to rape *her*?'

The jury were out for a day and a half. During that time, the media contingent floated around waiting for something to happen, while I sat in the CTV room with Tony and Kevin and Rebecca and Sheridan playing UNO. We played UNO for a day and a half, and it was actually great fun – I even beat the police officers a couple of times (I never let them hear the end of that). It was the perfect way to keep my mind off the stress of waiting. I was so anxious about what the jury was going to say that I couldn't eat or sleep. I kept going over everything in my head: was there anything I missed out, was there anything I forgot, was there anything that I needed to tell them, was there anything that I got mixed up? I wanted to bust into the jury room and tell them all the things they didn't know: that Kerry had set me up, that she was their friend, that she'd stolen my underwear from my bag in an attempt to destroy the evidence. None of that had been mentioned in court, so they didn't know any of it. Her version of events had pretty much been allowed to stand, even though it was completely untrue. I had so many thoughts running through my head I felt like I was going crazy. So that's why I was happy to sit there playing UNO – for those brief few seconds while I was thinking about what card I should put down next, I wasn't thinking about the jury.

The day the verdict came in, Tony drove me into court.

'Tony, what's going to happen?' I asked him. 'Do you think it's going to happen, is he going to get found guilty?'

'I don't know,' Tony said. 'But what you've got to remember is that Sabir's been charged with four different counts. The best that we can hope for is that we're going to get one count. We can't guarantee that we're going to get all of them. The best we can hope for is one. Don't get your hopes up.'

Finally, we were told the jury were ready to give their verdict. We were all called into the courtroom, and the media came flocking in from all corners of the planet. The courtroom was packed. The judge came out and the jury were called in. The only person who was missing was Sabir – he'd decided he didn't want to be there to hear the verdict, he wanted to hear it later.

All I really wanted to know was whether Sabir was guilty or not guilty, but there was a lot of legal mumbo jumbo to get through first. I was so impatient I hardly listened to everything leading up to it, but finally we got down to business.

The brothers had been charged with a joint criminal enterprise, which meant that they were all equally responsible for the four acts of sexual assault committed on the night (one act of digital penetration and three acts of penile penetration). Amir and Mustapha's trials had been aborted, so Sabir was facing all four charges alone. Whatever happened today he was going back to jail. He was already doing 22 years for the rape of the other two girls. But it was really important to me that he should be found guilty for what he'd done to me too. I wanted public acknowledgement that what he'd done to me was wrong and I wanted to see him punished for it, even if it was only on one or two counts. Four would be better. But I'd take whatever I could get.

The foreman was asked about the first charge.

The answer came back: 'Guilty.'

I was so happy I took this great big sigh of relief. I just wanted to do cartwheels in my seat. I was ecstatic.

The foreman was asked about the second charge. 'Guilty.'

The third charge. 'Guilty.'

The fourth charge. 'Guilty.'

He'd been found guilty on all four charges!

It was 14 June 2005. They'd raped me exactly three years before. It seemed like poetic justice that the verdict was handed down on that day.

I could *not* believe it. I was so happy. I wanted to run over and hug the jury, every single one of them. I wanted to let them know that it was absolutely awesome what they'd done for me, that they'd made the right decision, and that they'd done a huge favour to me and all the other girls who could've been raped by these guys. It was awesome.

Sheridan then sent me to wait outside while Sabir was brought up from the cells to hear the verdict. It would have been kind of satisfying to see his face as he realised he'd lost, but that didn't really matter to me. What mattered was that I'd won.

I went outside and started jumping around. I was so excited I wanted to go running up and down the hallways of the court. I was practically dancing for joy.

I saw one of the reporters from Channel 10, and was talking to her about how fantastic it was and how happy I was with the verdict. We saw a prison car drive past while we were talking, and she asked, 'What would you do if they were in that car right now?'

And I was so excited I shouted, 'Fuck you arsehole, I won, woo-hoo!'

The reporter cracked up laughing, and then we both stood there, yelling at the car and dancing around smiling. It was just so awesome. Everybody around me was really happy for me. They didn't need to be told what had happened. They could see that justice had been done. Sabir had been found guilty, and he was the one I really wanted to get.

Of course, I still had two to go. That was a bit scary, but after the outcome with Sabir, I didn't see how anything could go wrong with the other two. If the evidence had been strong enough to convict Sabir, it had to be strong enough to convict Amir and Mustapha. Right?

# 15

# Soft

A WEEK AFTER SABIR was found guilty, Amir and Mustapha appeared before Justice Hidden alone. Amir pleaded guilty to one count of Aggravated Sexual Assault, which carries a maximum penalty of twenty years' imprisonment. Two other charges were dropped, to save me from giving evidence again for what would probably end up as little, if any, extra sentence.

At the time, I found this kind of hard to take. It didn't seem fair to me that two of the charges were dropped, giving him a discount on his sentence. You're only supposed to get that benefit if you've saved everybody the expense of going to trial, not to mention saving the victim from the stress of having to give evidence. Amir didn't plead guilty until after everything was over and his brother had already been found guilty on all charges. I was still hopeful that we could have got him on all the charges, too. But it didn't happen that way.

Then it was Mustapha's turn. Justice Hidden looked at all the evidence he'd been presented with, and he decided that he couldn't convict. Mustapha was the only one who'd used a condom, so there wasn't any DNA evidence. Kerry and Sophie had managed to confuse things as well. Kerry had said Mustapha never left the room, Sophie said he only left the room for about two minutes. And his barrister had thrown doubt on my identification of him by saying that I couldn't have recognised him because the lights were off. He said I'd identified him by voice recognition alone and that that wasn't a strong enough identification.

That was completely wrong! It was so much more than voice recognition! The lights may have been off until he got up and switched them on again, but I saw Mustapha and I recognised him. I saw his face, I recognised his smell, I recognised his body shape. I saw him with his pants around his ankles pulling a used condom off his dick and dropping it on the floor. I was able to pick him out when the police showed me photos of him later. I was very, very clear about it. But it wasn't enough for Justice Hidden. He found him not guilty.

And that was crushing, because Mustapha was the worst of them. He slapped me across the face three times, threatened to stab me, told me he was fucking horny, pushed me onto a couch. He was so violent he left bruising. I don't think I would have had so many issues afterwards if it had just been the other two, because they weren't as violent, and I kept blacking out while they were raping me. But Mustapha was the most violent, the most scary, and I remember it much more clearly than the other two. I still carry the memories of what he did to me, and I'm still living with the effects. If I'm around guys who are drunk or too loud, guys who bump into me or even just brush past me without realising it, if they make loud noises or make any sudden moves, I still jump ten feet in the air. I can't help it. All the feelings of fear come back, even now. And that's because of Mustapha.

I firmly believe the jury would have found him guilty if they'd been given a chance, but thanks to Sabir that didn't happen. Mustapha got away with it. He was still going back to jail for the rape of the other two girls. But he raped me and threatened me and he got away with it.

When I heard the judgment I was devastated. Devastated and furious. Mustapha was gloating and I couldn't stand being in the same room with him one second longer. I jumped up and pushed past everyone and ran into the foyer and fell down in a heap and started to cry. Tony was there with me that day, and he was amazing.

He took me across the street to get coffee, and while we were sitting there, talking about the case, Mustapha's defence team walked in: an old man who looked like a broken teddy bear and a very unfashionable woman who really needed to do something about her appearance, lugging their court suitcases. They noticed me as they walked in and I gave them such a dirty look they turned around and walked out again, which was a pity, because I would have liked to have the chance to ask them how it felt to be keeping rapists out of prison.

After they'd gone Tony said something I'll never forget.

'This really sucks,' he said. 'But try and think of it like this. There's a thing called persistence of vision. When you blink and you close your eyes you actually lose a fraction of a second of what you see. But your brain stitches it together, so it all flows and you don't remember what you missed. Your brain makes a coherent story out of a whole sequence of little moments. That's pretty much what's happened here. Some things have been left out and the judge and the lawyers have patched together a story, and because things have been left out, that was enough to create reasonable doubt. That doesn't mean the things that were left out of the story didn't happen. They did happen. It's just the courts couldn't see them. Reasonable doubt means they couldn't find him guilty. That doesn't mean he's innocent. It just means he's not guilty.'

And that really helped me. It helped give a bit of meaning to what had just happened. It helped me put things in perspective.

Most people wouldn't expect to get emotional support from a couple of police officers, but for me, they were better than any counsellors. They had the knowledge and the experience to really understand what I was going through, and they knew exactly what to say. I'll always be grateful to both of them for the way they helped me. They were absolute legends the whole way through.

I don't feel the same way about Justice Hidden. I reckon he could have seen the good side of any criminal. But in the end, I think I was lucky that he allowed the charges against Sabir to go to the jury, because at least we got that conviction. I firmly believe the jury would have found Amir and Mustapha guilty too, if they'd been given a chance. In my opinion, Justice Hidden was out of touch with reality. I just don't think he understood what it's like to be a victim of one of these crimes. If he did, he couldn't be so soft on the people who perpetrate them.

# 16

# The HSC

THE FIRST THING THEY tell you at the start of Year 12 is that this year is the most important year of your life and you'll have to work harder than you ever have before because your future depends on how well you do in your exams.

The second thing they tell you is that even though your entire future is hanging in the balance, you should try not to get too stressed about it.

They didn't have any advice for what you should do if you're trying to conduct a court case in the middle of your Higher School Certificate. Here's my advice: don't try it.

My HSC subjects were English, Art, Drama, Studies of Religion, Family and Community Studies, and Legal Studies.

When I was choosing my subjects I had to think hard about what to choose. I chose Art and Drama for obvious reasons: I loved them. English was compulsory. I picked Legal Studies because I thought it would help me get a better understanding of the legal system and court proceedings. Even though I knew we'd be studying my case – I'd been told all about it by the girls who'd studied it the year before – I decided to do it anyway, because I thought it might give me some useful insights into the legal process. I chose Family and Community Studies because I thought it might help me understand my own situation a bit better; but I have to admit I also chose it because I thought it was a soft subject. I'd always loved science, but I suspected I was going to want some cruisy subjects to pad out my schedule. So science was out and Family Studies was in. I also took Studies of Religion, which gave me an interesting perspective on the whole 'Islam is evil' argument that was raging in the media.

Maybe I was stupid to try and do my HSC when I knew I'd have the ongoing stress and disruption of a court case. But I had a lot of good reasons for wanting to do it.

First, no girl in my family had ever got her HSC, and I wanted to be the first to do it. I knew if I didn't, my little sister would, and I had to maintain my perfect record of doing everything before her!

Second, people kept telling me I couldn't do it. I've been struggling with a reading and writing disability since I was a little girl, and a lot of people close to me – Mum, Nan –

thought I wouldn't be able to cope. Mum thought it was all going to be too hard for me and that I should give up, leave school and do something else. That's what she did – she did everything the hard way but still became a nurse. But I didn't want to do what my mum had done, I wanted to make my own way, so that made me even more determined to do it. If you want to guarantee I'll do something, tell me I can't. Then get out of the way.

And finally, Mustapha had done his HSC in prison. If he could do his HSC in prison, then I had to do mine while going to court.

And besides, what was I going to do if I left school? Sit around at home watching daytime television and stressing about what was going to happen? Go out and get a job? I wasn't qualified for anything, I wouldn't have been able to take on a traineeship because of my court commitments. I probably would have ended up working in a juice bar, which is not exactly stimulating, and there's no way I could have got the time off that I needed for the court case. So despite all the problems I had with school and all the people in it, school really was the best option for me.

School kept me in touch with what was going on in the world outside of Teganland. Teganland was court cases, trying to get a job, trying to deal with bulimia, trying not to cut myself, trying to have some sort of normal life. Trying to have a normal relationship with my mum. Missing my brothers and sisters chronically (I now had a second sister). Trying to hold on to memories of my dad. That's what I was dealing with in Teganland, so it was nice to step out of Teganland and step into school. Despite all the dramas and the bitchy comments, compared to Teganland, school was a breeze.

I went into my HSC hoping I'd be able to get through all my units and actually make a go of it, but it turned out to be much harder than I expected.

To begin with, there was the time I spent going to court. Every time I went I missed school, so that meant I was always missing out on things and having to catch up. But that wasn't my biggest problem. Even when I *was* at school, I wasn't always fully present. The stress and anxiety of having the court proceedings endlessly delayed by the boys and their stupid tactics, the worry of not knowing whether we would ever get to trial, and if we did, whether we'd get a conviction or not, was a constant distraction. If you want to do well in your HSC, you need to be able to clear your head of distracting thoughts and distracting emotions and just focus on your studies. There may be people out there who can block out stressful events by throwing themselves into work or study, but I'm not one of those people. The court case was simply too big and too important for me to be able to push it aside and not think about it. It wasn't quite *all* I could think about. But it came close.

Art and drama were an escape for me because they gave me a creative outlet for all my anger and frustration – especially art. Both subjects have a theoretical and a practical component, and they also require you to do a major project which you create on your own. My major art piece developed from an initial drawing I made of a set of lips. They were a Mick Jagger, Rolling Stones-inspired set of lips, and I developed that image further, making it a little scarier, adding a pair of eyeballs and a tongue ring, and giving it a frightened kind of look. In the whites of the eyeballs you could see a reflection that said 'the end'. I developed the idea further and created a painting that used a collection of images I'd been working on: a series of roads, which came together to form a tree; lots of eyes; street signs that had been altered and mutilated, saying things like 'stop' and 'go faster'. Winding around it was blue-and-white police crime scene tape, and in one corner was a hand holding a sheriff's badge.

Creating the piece was an interesting process for me because I didn't stop to analyse why I was using these sorts of images. They just felt right to me. It wasn't until Mr H said to me, 'Tegan, do I really have to read your own artwork for you?' that I realised what the piece was about. The roads, twisting and tangling and branching off, represented the journey I'd been on towards the court case. My sketchbooks were full of eyes because every time I went to court I felt like I was being scrutinised by everybody: the lawyers, the judge, the jury, the reporters. And those street signs saying stop, go, go faster, represented my contradictory feelings about the case. I was desperate for it to be over (stop), I was sick of all the delays (go faster), I was dying to see the boys safely in jail where they belonged (go – that is, to jail). The sheriff's badge was a reference to Tony and Kevin, the police officers who'd been in charge of my case and who were there in court with me every day. They both wore these tiny little badges on their blazers – I think they were detectives' badges – and they were incredibly proud of them. They were always fiddling with them and adjusting them. One day, one of them wore the wrong jacket to court and left his badge at home and he was incredibly cut up about being without it. So I put a huge sheriff's badge into my artwork as a tribute to them and their itty-bitty badges.

Someone came up to me once when I was working on my piece and asked, 'Do you take acid?'

'No,' I said. 'Why?'

'Because that piece is seriously trippy.'

And I guess if you don't know how to read it, it probably just looks like a really weird bunch of things all jumbled up together. But when I look at that painting, it's like looking at a map of everything I was thinking and feeling at the time.

Drama, although I loved it, was more problematic. You have to do an Individual Project – I performed a monologue – but you also have to do a Group Performance, and that was difficult because group rehearsals didn't fit in well with my court schedule.

Working on my monologue was easy because I could do it in my own time. My friend and I collaborated on the piece I performed, which was about a crazy girl. She doesn't realise she is crazy: she thinks she is going to a doctor's appointment and somehow she ends up in a white padded room, but she doesn't realise she's in the mental hospital, she just thinks it's a nice little place to sit, like a fashion closet. She decides the clothes she's wearing are fashionable, and that she's going to be appearing in a fashion show soon, but she can't quite work out what's going on, since people keep walking through walls and stuff like that. It was pretty freaky. I scared a few people when I performed it.

For our Group Performance we had to devise and write a group piece, then rehearse and perform it. I was off in court while we were supposed to be working on our piece, so every time we tried to rehearse I was either away in court, or just back from court and stressed out over what had happened, which made it really difficult to get anything done. This didn't just affect me; it affected everybody in my group. If we couldn't rehearse properly, everybody's mark would suffer, not just mine. Drama is very competitive and it can get very bitchy and we didn't have an easy time getting our piece together, but we managed it in the end.

Our Group Performance was an absurdist piece about a whole group of characters trying to work out how they fitted into society. We devised it as a group and it was very long and tiring to perform. The script was put together out of things we came up with ourselves plus lines and quotes that came from other things, particularly from songs that were mean-ingful to us, like Queen songs or songs from the musical *Rent*.

My uncle had a catchphrase that he used all the time – 'Stop the world, I want to get off' – and that idea became part of our piece. One of the big influences on the piece was a song called 'Coin-Operated Boy' which we used to create one of our main characters, a little girl from a broken home, and she coped with the break-up of her parents' marriage by investing all her emotions in this coin-operated boy instead. We had another character, a boy who was a social outcast: he was gay, he dressed like a girl, he was an absolute nutball and he found it impossible to fit in.

My character was a complete know-it-all, a walking dictionary. My character thought she had the answers to everything, and every time something went wrong for the two central characters, my character would tell them exactly what it meant and what she thought about it and what they should do about it. My character was a bit of a smart-arse, but really she didn't know what she was talking about. She knew nothing. And just occasionally she'd have these moments when she'd know she was talking absolute garbage, and she'd wonder whether everyone around her realised how full of crap she really was or whether she was managing to fool them. My character was one of those people who are always trying to pretend they're something they're not instead of just being themselves.

My character wasn't me, but there were parallels with what was going on in my own life. Going to court is a very confusing business; there's a lot of stuff that goes right over your head, so often when I was up on the stand or sitting in court listening to the lawyers talk I really felt like I was winging it – I don't mean I was lying, but it often felt like a real struggle to understand what was going on. People were bombarding me with questions, and I had to sound like I was sure of the answers, even if I wasn't, because if I showed any sort of hesitation or weakness at all, they'd pounce.

The time I spent in court made it difficult enough to keep up with my schoolwork. But the thing that made it really hard was the fact that as the year went on I began to feel like everything I was studying was commenting on some aspect of my life. It began to feel like, 'What the hell? Is this some kind of conspiracy theory?' Because all my subjects seemed to be about me, sometimes in the most literal way.

I'd taken Legal Studies because I thought it would help me understand what was going on with my own case – and it did give me some understanding, but not in a good way. One of the things it did was show me how unfair the legal system can be, how hard it can be on victims, and how gruelling the process can be. We studied other rape cases and it became very clear to me that the process of going to court was really traumatic for the victims, and sometimes you didn't even get a conviction, and there were a million ways it could all go wrong and you would have gone through all that trauma for nothing. And so I'd be sitting there in class wondering, is that what's going to happen to me? It was bad enough that I had to wait – and wait – and wait for anything to happen with my case. Sitting in a classroom thinking about how horrible it was going to be just made it that much harder.

I think my Legal Studies teacher began to wish he didn't have me in his class, because I kept asking really awkward questions. We'd be talking about a case, and I'd say, 'Yes, but sir, the lawyers are there to protect the accused, not the victim. The victim doesn't have any rights at all.' And the rest of the class would start wanting to know why victims didn't have any rights and why the accused gets all the protection, until I think my teacher was wishing he could just make me go away. Because I was bringing up really difficult issues, and the reason I knew they were difficult was because I was going through them. And there aren't any easy answers to them.

In the end I found Legal Studies too much to deal with and I stopped going to class. Whenever I had Legal Studies I'd head off to the art room and tell Mr H I had a study period so I could work on my art. You'd think he would have noticed I was having an awful lot of study periods, but if he did, he didn't say anything. I guess he thought it was better that I was working on something rather than just skipping school completely.

For someone who spent so much time hanging out in court with lawyers, you'd think I would've got good marks in Legal Studies, but I probably hold the title as worst student ever. I think I came last. When it came to the final exam, I wrote a grand total of ten words on the paper and that was it, I was done. I sat there for the rest of the three hours and drew on my exam paper. I was very artistic. I gave them a wonderful drawing.

Community and Family Studies was another subject that hit a little too close to home. I went into it thinking it was a bit of a wishy-washy subject that wouldn't be too much of a stretch, but I soon found it all a bit too much to cope with. Basically it looked at different kinds of families and different groups within the community, particularly the kinds of groups who were on the outer, like gay people, the homeless, the mentally ill. It also looked at issues like divorce and family breakdown. Obviously that was all pretty personal for me: although I didn't exactly come from a broken home, my family life had always been a bit unconventional, and since the rapes, my relationship with my grandparents had become very strained. And while I was hanging out with the friends I met through the refuge, I'd had a taste of what it was like to live on the fringes of society. People used to cross the street to avoid us when they saw us coming. We were noisy and stupid and didn't care what people thought of us. For a while I hadn't cared – it was kind of fun acting like a menace to society. But now I'd grown out of that, and taking Community and Family Studies was kind of an uncomfortable experience for me because it made me feel like I'd been a complete loser. It felt like yet another subject where I was being asked to answer questions and write assignments about my own life, and it was all too raw and too real and too personal for me to be able to look at it objectively and treat it as just another subject.

Although some of the things I learnt in Community and Family Studies were useful to me – particularly in Drama, where I was able to use some of the ideas from that course in our Group Performance – as the year wore on I began to wish I'd made different choices. Like, why didn't I pick Hospitality? I could've learnt to cook and developed some real skills, without ever having to worry about it bringing back painful memories. Cooking has no bad associations. But I didn't foresee any of that.

Looking back now I can see it was never really going to work. All I could think about that year was the court case. From February until June I was constantly shuttling off to court. In August, the fourth girl's case went to trial. In October, while final exams were on, I was back in court reading my victim impact statement for Amir's sentencing hearing.

I was excited about giving my victim impact statement to the court, but terrified too. Excited because for the first time I could speak freely about what had happened – I could get up and tell my side of the story, without being questioned or called a liar or being made out to be promiscuous, and everyone had to listen to what I had to say. All three of the boys were there – Sabir and Amir for me, Mustapha for the fourth victim – and I got to look them right in the eye and make them pay attention while I told them, 'This is what you did to me.'

I was terrified that if I left out anything important, the judge might stand up and say, 'Well, it could've been a lot worse. See you later boys, you're free to go.'

As usual with the courts, there was a lot of legal rigmarole to get through first. Then I got up and read my victim impact statement – it was a shorter version of this book. Then the fourth victim's mum got up and read a statement about what that rape had done to her daughter and her family.

Then as we were leaving I had a stand-off with Dr K – the boys' father. It was the first time I'd ever seen him, since he wasn't at the trials. This time he was there with his wife. The courtroom separates the defence side from the prosecution side, and each has their own door. The two doors face each other across a tiny little vestibule, so if two people come out of the doors at the same time, there's really only room for one person to get out at a time. And I chose to leave the courtroom at the same moment as Dr K. He knew exactly who I was of course, and I could see he thought I should get out of his way. But I stood my ground, and for a moment the two of us just stared at each other. That stare – if I was the kind of person to be scared, I would have been packing it. I can only describe it as a cold, wide-eyed, evil stare. He put on the best Satan impression. But then I went through the door, and that was that. I never saw him again.

I was back in court again in December for Sabir's sentencing hearing. If those boys didn't get found guilty, I was going to go insane, and that was probably the hardest part about the whole situation: it felt like my whole life depended on the verdict.

And that made it impossible to relax, or think about other stuff, or even just be normal. I couldn't sit around with my friends and laugh about stupid things we'd read in magazines. I couldn't learn what the teachers were trying to teach me. The only choice I had was to go to school and sit there like a mindless drone, or go to court and just stare at the boys and let them know that I was there and that I wasn't going to let them beat me.

So how did I do? I got a UAI (Universities Admission Index) of 35 per cent. It's not as bad as it sounds – I got in the 80s for Drama and the 90s for Art. But the Board of Studies scales both those subjects down, so I ended up with 35 per cent. But at least I made it through the year. I finished my HSC, in spite of everything and everyone.

With a score like that I wasn't going to be heading straight off to uni. But I didn't care. I needed some time to stop and take stock, get myself a job, and think about what I wanted to do with the rest of my life.

And besides, I still had to find out what the boys' sentences were going to be. Had it all been worthwhile? Were they going to get what they deserved? Or was it going to be one more disappointment?

# 17

# Life after school

I'D ALWAYS DREAMED OF becoming an early childhood teacher, so as soon as the HSC was over I started applying for jobs working with kids.

I soon found one, working as a trainee pre-school teacher. I was thrilled to be out of school, doing something I loved – working with little kids – and making a start on a new life. But I soon began to realise that the reality of the job was a long way from what I'd imagined.

As a trainee, I'd hoped that I'd get to spend a reasonable amount of time with the kids themselves. I love kids – you don't go into that field for any other reason, you're certainly not going to get rich that way. But I found I was spending nearly all my time working as a cleaner. Every day I had a huge round of chores to get through before there was even a possibility that I might get to spend some time with the kids. And even if I did get my chores done, my boss would always find something else for me to do. I was like Cinderella trying to get all these impossible tasks done so she could go to the ball. And when I did get to spend time with the kids, it was not an ideal situation. The group I was working with were kids aged between two and three, but many of them were closer to two than three. They were still really little and needed a lot of attention. There are strict rules about staff ratios in childcare centres: at that age, there is supposed to be about one staff member to every eight kids, and trainees are not supposed to be in charge of kids without a fully qualified staff member present. But when the kids went down for their naps I'd frequently be left with one other trainee in charge of a sleep room with about 30 kids in it. And if you know anything about kids, you know that when you put them down to sleep they don't always go to sleep.

I worked from seven in the morning until six-thirty at night, often without a break, cooking, cleaning, tidying up. Some days when I was putting the kids to sleep I'd be having a hard time staying awake myself because I was so exhausted.

The last straw came one day when I'd worked especially hard to get through all my jobs so I could spend a bit of time with the kids. I was hoping I might be able to do what I was there to do: learn. But when my boss saw that I'd finished everything she pulled out a crucifix and said to me, 'We're having an Easter Mass – I need you to polish this for me. You can go to my office and polish it.' That was it for me. I was like, 'Right, okay, we're done. No more.' I went home that night and got out the phone book and started at A and I rang every childcare centre until I found one that was willing to give me a job.

The next day I walked into my boss's office and said, 'Look, I'm not happy with this. I didn't take this job to be a cleaner. The other day I finished everything and you made me polish a crucifix.'

She stood up then – she's quite a big lady – and stood over me and said, 'I'm sorry if I want my children's mass to be perfect. You're a selfish little brat, and when I ask you to do something I expect you to do it. That's what I'm employing you for.'

'Listen here, lady,' I said. 'I'm not a little kid, I'm not one of your students, you can't push me round and sit me in the naughty chair. So this is what I'm going to say to you: my cooling-off period ended today. I'm walking out. I'm going. If you're nice to me I might give you two weeks' notice to get another trainee in. If you're not nice, by the end of the day I'm taking my stuff and leaving.' And then I said, 'Oh and by the way, I'm not a cleaner, I'm a pre-school teacher. I don't clean crosses for the fun of it, I work with kids for the fun of it.' That was it for me. I wasn't going to be pushed around by this woman. I told her I was leaving.

After that, she took my theory work and the modules I was supposed to be doing for my traineeship and she hid them from me. She actually took my work out of the office and took it back to her house and she wouldn't let me leave until seven o'clock that night. Needless to say, I never went back.

I called the people who were running my traineeship and told them what had happened and they told me she was just being a bully. So I called Work Relations and told them everything. They told me that that she owed me about a thousand dollars because of all the missed breaks. I thought about sending her a letter and demanding back pay, but I knew I'd never see any of the money, and it wasn't really worth all the drama, so I let it go. Still, sometimes I check up on the internet to see if she has advertising up. She advertises for new staff every week.

My next job was at a much better centre. The people were great and I loved working with the kids. But I got off to an incredibly difficult start because the week I started work was the week of the sentencing, and I hadn't told them about it. One day, I was just a new trainee, the next day I was the public face of rape. After I came out to the media I had to ring work and say, 'Look, this has just happened, it's about to be all over the media, but I really want this job.'

I got off to a pretty bumpy start in that job, because all the media were chasing me for interviews. I switched my phone off but they found out where I worked and started ringing the centre. They came around with cameras wanting to interview me. You can just imagine how impressed my new employer was about that.

Once all the excitement had died down a bit I really tried to settle in and do the best job I could. But after a while I began to realise that there were a number of things about the childcare business that were quite frustrating. Looking after other people's children is, of course, a very responsible job. But the fact is, kids sometimes fall over, and they do sometimes hurt themselves. It's part of life, it's how they learn. But you're always living in terror of being sued.

You also have to do a lot of tiptoeing around the parents. I found that pretty difficult. Every parent thinks their child is uniquely special and talented. And every child *is* special, but not every child is a genius. And you just can't say that to a parent.

I began to realise this job wasn't going to work out for me. I was also still getting a lot of phone calls from the media while I was supposed to be working, so eventually my boss called me in and suggested that maybe I should take some time off until I got my life sorted out and I worked out exactly what it was I wanted to do. So I took that advice, and once I was away from the job I began to realise it really wasn't right for me. Apart from anything else I've got a reading and writing disability – how am I going to teach kids to read and write if I have problems doing it myself? And much as I enjoyed spending time with kids, I found it wasn't as challenging as I'd expected. So that was the end of that dream.

And after eleven years of living with my nan, I decided it was time to get a place of my own. It was an amazing feeling the first time I walked into my own place, with my own things, and I knew that I could have it exactly the way I wanted it. My place, my rules. No one could ever kick me out or make me feel unwelcome.

Moving out was a big step for me. It meant independence; it meant I was finally growing up. And for the first time it meant I didn't have to hide anything from my nan. If I wanted to see a guy, I didn't have to sneak out of the house and meet him in the street. I could just invite him in without having to go through the hassle of introducing him to my grandparents and having them ask him a ton of embarrassing questions.

I started sneaking out to see boys when I was still pretty young – it was one of the things I used to do with Selina and Margaret. Some of those boys were friends, and some of them were more than friends. I don't know if hooking up with a guy is more complicated for me than it is for everybody else. From what I've heard, everybody has times when it's weird or embarrassing or kind of gross. That's one of the things people want to know about after you've been raped, but they're afraid to ask: what does it do to your relationships? Are you still interested in boys? Can you still have sex? I can't answer for everyone, but in my case the answer is definitely yes. Everybody has to learn how it's done. I had to learn too – I'm a normal girl, it's just that I had this horrible early experience to get past before I could enjoy it. There's stuff I won't ever want to do (which is why it was so ridiculous that Sabir tried to pretend I'd offered to do it 69-style with him – is there any woman who really likes to do that? I mean, *really*?). But I don't think the rapes have scarred me for life.

There are things that frighten me, and probably always will. If someone starts acting aggressively or violently, even if they're only playing around, I can't deal with that, I'm out of there. If I ask someone not to do something and they do it anyway, I can't cope with that either. I have to feel like I'm being respected and listened to and that I can control what's happening. But I suspect there are plenty of girls out there who've never been raped who feel the same way.

Sudden or unexpected moves of a sexual kind can scare me too. Once when I was still at school I was sitting with my friend and her boyfriend. They were hooking up and I was just zoning out, away in Teganland. Suddenly, the boyfriend put his hand on my inner thigh and said, 'Your turn.' He was joking, but in the first moment I didn't realise that, and it frightened me so much I jumped 50 feet in the air and pushed him away with both hands. It was only then that I realised he'd been kidding and I had to pretend I'd just been mucking around too, and that I hadn't completely freaked out.

I haven't got a great track record in picking guys. For some reason I seem to attract abusive boyfriends. Not always physically abusive, but guys who want to put women down. It's not obvious at first, and as soon as I realise what they're like I ditch them. I'm not stupid, I don't seek them out, but for some reason I just seem to keep finding them. It's ridiculous. Maybe it has something to do with my dad dying so young and my mum being – well, my mum – so I don't really have a good sense of what a functional relationship is like. (Obviously my grandparents have a functional relationship, but they're my *grandparents*.) Maybe it's just me. Either way, I hope my taste improves.

My past may not have affected me much when it comes to relationships, but it has been difficult for a number of guys to deal with. Some of the people I've been involved with have known about it. Others haven't. There was one guy I saw for a while, and I never told him about the rapes. A long time after we'd broken up he saw me on TV and he got in contact with me again. 'I think I just saw you,' he said. 'Was that you? Why didn't you tell me?'

All I could say was, 'What was I supposed to tell you?'

Our relationship didn't last long – he was nice, but we just weren't compatible. I suppose if we'd stayed together there would have been a moment when it seemed right to tell him. But when's the right time? Too early and you'll freak them out, too late and you'll hurt their feelings for not telling them sooner. Sometimes you just think, why complicate things?

Some guys can't cope with what happened to me at all. Just recently there was someone I was kind of involved with – he was a friend, and I really wanted us to be more. And one day things started to heat up between us, but then he said, 'So are you going to turn around and tell people I raped you too?'

I couldn't believe it. It ended in a huge fight, and I decided then and there that he wasn't worth the time and effort. The last thing he said to me as I was kicking him out the door was, 'Why don't you go fuck some Pakis?'

I'd started seeing another guy at the time of the sentencing. We hadn't been together for long – in fact, we weren't officially seeing each other – and so I wasn't sure how he'd react to the media interest. I talked to him about the possibility of telling my story. He didn't want me to talk about it at all – he was a fairly selfish person – but I told him I'd made up my mind and that it needed to be done. For one day – literally one day – he was okay with it. But then the rest of our group of friends found out about it – they couldn't miss it, it was all over the news – and after that, it all went wrong. He didn't want to be seen in public with me. He'd only hang out with me at home when there was no one there. He was ashamed of me. He actually told me that. I probably should have blown him off right then, but I didn't. One day a reporter called and asked me to do an interview for a story they were doing. It was an important subject and I really wanted to do it, but he made me feel incredibly bad about it, and it quickly turned into a fight. He accused me of being an attention seeker. I told him the media attention would die down soon, that it would probably only last a month or so and this interview was the last one I was likely to do.

'Right,' he said, 'so you decided to go out with one big bang, did you?'

I was really hurt by that. And it wasn't because I thought he was The One and I had all these big plans for our future together. I was just so upset that someone I'd liked and respected could say something like that to me.

We went our separate ways after that.

So I haven't been lucky with men. But hopefully I'm getting better at separating the nice guys from the arseholes. When I find the right person I'd like to have kids – maybe when I'm 30 or 35, that seems like a good age to me. There's a lot I want to do with my life first, so I'll just have to wait and see how that dream turns out.

# 18

# Have fun, boys

ON 6 APRIL 2006 I went back to court for the last time. I'd been waiting for this day for close to four years. I was going to hear the boys' sentences.

I made sure I was early to court that day. I didn't want to miss a thing. I sat down in the very front row of the public gallery so the boys wouldn't possibly be able to miss me. At ten o'clock the three of them were brought into the dock, all dressed in their dark suits. It wasn't such a shock seeing them this time, but it still gave me a bit of a jolt. Sabir mouthed 'I'm sorry' to me, but I didn't want to know. Too little, too late. Way too late. Amir was sitting next to him, and he looked like he was actually insane, because he was talking to himself.

I watched him for a while and he wasn't talking to his brothers or praying. My family's the God squad; I can tell when someone's praying, and he definitely wasn't. He would say something and then pause and then say something and then pause, as if he could hear someone responding. I was like, okay, maybe you should have had that insanity plea and not your brother. Mustapha just kept shaking his head at me, as if to say, 'I'm so disappointed in you.' It just reminded me – not that I needed reminding – how much I hated him.

Then the judge arrived, and a court official began reading the charges. I'd brought my flatmate with me and she'd never been to anything like this before. She was seriously shocked when they started chucking around terms like 'digital pene-tration'. I was just thinking, oh, come on, guys, do you have to? but she turned to me and said, '*What* did he just say?' It was so clinical and so precise. But that's the court system for you. They've got to spell everything out.

Not that they made everything clear. Oh no. They use so many big words and so much legalistic terminology it's incredibly hard to follow what they're saying. Now, I can talk for a very long time without taking a breath, I can use a lot of big words, or I can talk really quick. But the legal jargon trotted out that day completely left me for dead. I was totally bewildered by what was going on. I had to turn to Tony, who was sitting next to me, and get him to translate it all for me.

Sabir was sentenced first. The previous October at the

sentencing hearing, after Sabir had been found guilty by the jury, he had found a barrister who was willing to get up and argue that the whole thing was a cultural misunderstanding. Where Sabir came from in Pakistan, teenage girls always wore veils and never hung out with members of the opposite sex unless they were chaperoned by a male member of their family. Because me and the other victims hadn't been wearing veils and hadn't been chaperoned, Sabir and his brothers had simply assumed that we were promiscuous and they could do what they liked with us. Justice Hidden said he'd given the matter serious consideration, but had decided it was all nonsense. The boys had spent enough time in Australia to understand the cultural norms here. They knew what they were doing was wrong, and they did it anyway.

Justice Hidden sentenced Sabir to serve five and a half years with a further non-parole period of three and a half years for my rape. That meant that he would serve a minimum of 22 years and a maximum of 26 years for the various rapes he'd committed.

Amir was next. After his part of the trial was aborted, he pleaded guilty to one count of Aggravated Sexual Assault. At the sentencing hearing, Amir had made a big show of being remorseful. I didn't buy it, but Justice Hidden did. He sentenced Amir to only nine years imprisonment for my rape, with a non-parole period of four years. But because Amir was already serving a minimum of twelve years and a maximum of sixteen years for the rape of the other two girls, that meant that with my rape included, he would serve a minimum of fourteen and a maximum of nineteen years.

Mustapha was last. Justice Hidden had already found him not guilty of raping me. He was there to be sentenced for having consensual sex with a minor, the fourth girl in our case. Justice Hidden was completely convinced by Mustapha and his team. He talked about Mustapha doing his HSC in jail, doing training courses, his positive prospects for rehabilitation. Had he been listening when I told him how Mustapha had hit me and threatened to stab me before brutally raping me? All Mustapha got was a twelve-month sentence to be served concurrently with the 22-year sentence he was already serving for the other rapes.

And that was it. Justice Hidden got up and left. The sentencing was over. I got up with my flatmate and Tony and Kevin and started walking for the door. And then it was like 'ding!' Suddenly it dawned on me that I didn't have to keep my mouth shut any longer. I didn't have to pretend to be a quiet, well-mannered young lady. I didn't have to worry about influencing the jury or annoying the judge or risking the outcome. It was over, done, finished.

'I'm going back in there for a minute, I'll be one second,' I said.

'Tegan, Tegan, don't do anything stupid,' said Kevin. 'Tegan, come back here.' And he turned to my flatmate and said, 'Quick, go follow her, make sure she doesn't do anything stupid.'

I walked back into the courtroom and said, 'Oi, have fun in prison. Fuck you. I hate you. You're arseholes.' And then I just stuck my finger up at them and said, 'Have fun in prison, boys – have fun.'

I'd been so good and so quiet for so long I think the boys were a bit dumbfounded that I'd finally said something to them, so none of them actually said anything back.

I know it was totally immature of me. But it was such a satisfying moment. I'm not someone who enjoys keeping their mouth shut and I'd had to stay quiet for four long years. Finally, I got to say what I really thought, and it felt amazing.

The courtroom was still full of reporters when I said it, and for a moment the whole room just stopped. Then it was like a bunch of seagulls jumping for a chip. The notepads and the tape recorders came out and they were all scrambling to write down what I said. And when I left the courtroom I saw there were even more reporters hanging around outside.

'They're here for you, Tegan,' Kevin said.

'Yeah, right,' I said. 'I bet they're here for some murder case that's been going on for the last six years.'

'No,' Kevin said, 'they're for you.'

There were reporters from the papers, from radio, from TV, there were microphones and cameras everywhere, all waiting for me. Rape victims usually have their identities suppressed, so I don't know what they thought they were going to get, but they were all there anyway. And a lot of them had seen me give the boys the finger. I guess they could tell I was in a feisty mood.

As we walked towards the waiting media, Kevin leaned over to me and said, 'Now remember, whatever you do, don't smile.' So what do I do? I start smiling. And then Tony said, 'And don't fall down the stairs.' So of course then I'm checking where I'm walking just to make absolutely sure I don't fall down the steps. All the cameras filmed the whole thing. Tony and Kevin made me look like a tool. But I couldn't complain – they'd been great through the whole thing.

As soon as I appeared, the journos all started yelling questions and asking me if I wanted to make a comment. Did I want to make a comment? You bet I did! I gave a full-on press conference right there on the steps of the court. I wanted the world to know that I wasn't ashamed to come forward. I won, so why should I hide?

I hadn't planned to make a statement. I hadn't thought about what I was going to say. But once I was there with all those cameras on me, I found it was easy.

They began by asking what I thought of the sentences.

'I wasn't too happy,' I said, 'but, I mean, it's the most I could've hoped for, I guess, in the scheme of things. I mean, I wasn't too impressed by it. I really thought they should've gotten more. But, hey, can't really do anything about it now.'

Seeing them sentenced had been incredibly satisfying, but seeing them given another twenty years would have been a lot *more* satisfying. Sabir got five and a half years for raping me. Amir got an extra three years. Mustapha got nothing. I know those sentences were loaded on top of the sentences they'd already been given, but to me that just didn't seem fair. It still doesn't. If they'd raped those other girls, served their fifteen years or whatever, got out of jail, and *then* raped me, they would have gone down for another fifteen years. But because they did them in sequence and got tried and sentenced for them in sequence, they got a discount. It's not exactly what you'd call a disincentive, is it? Commit multiple rapes and only get a few extra years tacked on to your sentence? Why not just go for it, see how many times you can get away with it before the police catch up with you.

I think the judge in the Skaf case who handed down those gigantic sentences had the right idea. Gang-rape seems to be turning into a trend now – 'Let's get all my buddies together and show them how manly I am.' Whatever happened to the days when they'd just show each other how manly they are by decking each other? They might break a bit of furniture but it's replaceable, it's not going to cause some woman a lifetime of trauma. Gang-rape is like the latest fashion for criminals and we've got to stamp it out before it gets any worse. I think judges need to put their foot down and say, 'You know what? We're not going to tolerate this crap. I'm going to make an example of you.' And hand down some serious penalties. Because if the courts are just going to give offenders a slap on the wrist for this sort of thing, then every time someone comes through the court system, even if the judge wants to give them a big sentence they can't, because the twenty guys before him only got a short amount of time. And that isn't right. Justice Hidden didn't do it for me, but I hope the next time one of these cases comes up, the judge stands up for the victims and gives the offenders a really serious sentence. Because no one's going to start taking any notice until they do.

In November 2006, the Crown successfully appealed Sabir's sentence and, all up, his maximum sentence was increased to 32 years, with a non-parole period of 24 years. The Crown also tried to appeal Amir and Mustapha's sentences but they were unsuccessful.

Still, Mustapha was going to be in jail for at least thirteen years. Amir was going to be in jail for at least fourteen years. Even though I would've liked to see them get more, in the original sentencing and after the appeal, I wasn't going to complain too much. They were off the streets and they wouldn't be able to hurt any more girls for a long time to come. That was an incredibly satisfying feeling.

Then one of the reporters asked me how I'd found the courage to stand up in court when so many victims won't. This is what I said.

'A lot of people come up to me and say, "How did you do it? You must have a heap of strength." But I actually don't believe that I really did have that much strength to do it. I just kind of did it.

'If I can do it, other girls can do it. I mean, it seems so

daunting at the time. You get told how long it's going to be between court dates, you get told all about things that are going to happen that you don't like, but at the end of the day it's worth it. You've just put these guys behind bars who now, because of you, can't hurt another woman, which is fantastic. I mean, all girls who are victims of assault should just come forward just for their own satisfaction. It's not good that they should be scared and hide and say, you know, "Maybe it was my fault," or anything like that. I mean, it's not right.

'The whole cultural issue wasn't an issue to begin with. With me, it wasn't. This wasn't about culture; this was about abuse against women. The fact that they had the nerve to bring in culture to begin with just astounds me.

'The reason I'm speaking out today is to tell other girls out there who have been rape victims or sexual assault victims of any description that it's not something you should be ashamed of, it's not something you should be scared of, and that you should come forward and for your own satisfaction and for your own – just for yourself, pretty much. Just go forward and do something about it.'

There was a lot more that I could have said. If you put me in a room with the boys now I'd have a lot more to say. First, there'd be a lot of profanities. Then, once I'd got that out of my system, I'd give them the benefit of my views on their characters. I'd tell them I think they need to grow up. That their views on women come from another age and it's really time they cleaned up their act. I'd tell them that when they picked on me they picked on the wrong girl. Did they ever choose the wrong girl!

But once I'd got all that off my chest, there are a few things I'd like to ask them. Why did you do this? Why did you rape all those girls? Why would you want to do that? And what was it about me that made you pick me?

And after that, I'd have a few more questions: Do you respect women? Do you think we're equal to you? Or do you think that you're better than me? I don't understand where this urge to hurt other people comes from. I would never do something so terrible to anybody. I know what it's like to be so angry you want to smash somebody – I've done it, I've got physical with people – but I learnt to overcome that urge. I am a human being. I have humanity, and a conscience; I would never do anything physically or mentally harmful to anyone. But that's what they did to me. And I'd want to ask them just how they thought they were going to get away with it. What on earth made them think I was going to let them get away with it?

That night I was on every TV news service, and I was on the front page of all the newspapers the next day. I was glad, because it meant that my message was getting out there. But if I'm honest, it was pretty satisfying for me personally, too. For one thing, I knew the boys would be watching from jail, and knowing it was me who put them there. For another, I'd had to put up with people calling me a liar for so many years, and now, finally, I'd been vindicated in the most public way. I'd won my case. It was in all the papers. Anyone who didn't believe me could read the reports and what the judge said. It was sweet revenge.

# 19

# My fifteen minutes

NOTHING I'D EVER DONE before had prepared me for my moment in the spotlight. Nobody had ever told me, for example, that when you're talking to a reporter, you're never just having a friendly chat. Ever. You have to be really careful what you say to them, because any of it – even if you say, 'This is off the record' – might pop up in a story later on. Nobody had even told me I could say, 'This is off the record' until I'd said all kinds of things I shouldn't have.

A number of reporters had followed my case from the start, and I'd got to know some of them over the course of the trial and the various hearings. I built up a great relationship with some of them. There was one female TV reporter who'd been a real support to me while I was giving evidence, because every time I looked at her she gave me such a bright sunny smile, and it made me feel like I must be going okay. She followed my case all the way through and we had a number of good chats while we were both hanging around waiting for things to happen. It never felt like she was pumping me for information about the case – I really felt she had a genuine interest in the case and was hoping to see me and the other victims get the best possible outcome. Needless to say, she got a lot of interviews out of me when it was all over. I also spent a lot of time hanging out with author and journalist Paul Sheehan, who was writing a book about the case. He'd been to every court date and watched all the boys' manoeuvring, and because he knew all about the case he helped explain what was going on, and didn't mind listening while I bitched. Unlike the other reporters he wasn't on deadline all the time so he had more time to talk, and also for him it wasn't just another court case. He really got involved and he really wanted to see justice done. That helped me a lot.

In general, though, the media are just feral when it comes to getting a story. There were two current affairs shows who went really hard to try and get me to speak to them exclusively. I let one of them do a story with me the day of the sentencing, and they came barging into my house and were incredibly rude and pushy. They wanted to do a story on the boys' father, Dr K, and they kept trying to get me to talk about him. Some allegations had been made against him and one of the boys –

not by me, but the reporter wanted me to confirm them. Obviously I wasn't in a position to do that – I hadn't made the allegations, I didn't know whether they were true or not; I had no business going on television and saying they were. If the girls who made the allegations wanted to repeat them on TV I was happy to stand by them and hold their hand, but it wasn't my place to jump in, uninvited, and start speaking for them. But the reporter wouldn't let it go. They'd already decided what they wanted me to say, so they kept pushing me until I said something they could use. And they kept asking me questions about it, and I kept trying to avoid them, and finally I said, 'If these allegations are true, then like father, like son.' Because I didn't want to get sued by Dr K. But when the interview ran, they'd edited out the part where I said, 'If these allegations are true.' All you got was me saying, 'Like father, like son,' as if it was all true. And then they asked me questions like, 'What did you think of Sabir?' And of course I started ranting about how much I hated him. 'He's a low-life and a cretin, he's a worthless piece of shit, he has no morals, blah blah blah.' And then when the interview went to air they changed the question to, 'So what do you think of Dr K?' I couldn't believe they'd do something like that. I was absolutely furious. So I decided to hit them where it hurts and refuse to give them any more stories and I'd give all my stories to the other show. That's how you hurt the media – you go to the competition. Suing them, that's not going to hurt them, they've got a billion dollars. Go to the competition. So much better. It's funny too because you get them to jump through hoops, they think that you're going to do the interview and then you're just like, gotcha.

The other show wasn't so bad. The only thing I wasn't happy about was when they called my work – but that was my problem more than theirs, because I hadn't told work yet. This is the way those big TV shows operate: they rang my work and told them, 'We'll pay you to employ someone else to take Tegan's place this afternoon, but we need you to let her out of work early.' They sent a car to pick me up and take me home so I could get changed, and then they sent a helicopter to fly me from my house to the studio. It wasn't like it was all that far from my place to the studio, but it was peak-hour traffic and they needed me to go live. That bit was fun.

My friends were all at the pub watching the show on TV. As the interview concluded, the interviewer asked me, 'Tegan, what are you going to go do now?'

I said, 'Oh, I think I'm just going to go home to reflect.'

Back at the pub my friends were all shouting, 'Bullshit!'

Once the interview was over I got them to drop me off at the pub. As soon as I walked in my friends were saying, 'Yeah, we knew you weren't going home to reflect.'

It was a strange time. People were ringing me up and offering to pay me large sums of money for an interview. I didn't take any in the end, but it was kind of cool getting the offers. I was thinking, you're offering me *how* much? But it was actually kind of bad, because I felt like I was being offered money to say things I didn't necessarily believe. At the time of the Cronulla riots I was offered quite a large sum of money to talk about Sheik Hilaly and his comment that women are like uncovered meat. I just didn't want to do it, because I didn't want my personal message to be misconstrued. What he said was wrong, and I think it's tragic that a whole generation of young men believe that this is the way things are between men and women. But I didn't want people to look at what I've been doing and start saying, 'It's all about race' as opposed to 'It's all about assault'. I didn't want people to think I was motivated by racism, because I'm not. I've never bought into the anti-Muslim thing. Australian guys rape women too.

I was asked to do a speech at the Reclaim the Night rally, and I was happy to do it, but then one of the current affairs shows got wind of it and said they'd fund all the rally's costs if I'd give them an interview. That left a bit of a bad taste in my mouth, because at the very beginning when I first met them they'd given me all these grand speeches about how they didn't pay people for interviews. But they *were* willing to give money to this cause I cared about if I'd do the interview, so of course I felt like I had to do the interview because I wanted to help out the rally organisers.

But the whole thing makes me a bit uncomfortable, because I don't want to turn into one of those people who's famous for being famous and who makes a living out of talking to the media. If the media have paid you however many thousands of dollars to tell your story, then somehow the story becomes about how much money you made, not what you've actually got to say.

I think it's one thing to sit down and write a book about your experiences; it's quite another to be handed a big wad of cash to sit down with a journalist for half an hour. One's about telling your story, the other's about exploiting yourself and letting other people exploit you. When I agreed to let the media print my name and use my face, I didn't do it because I thought it would make me rich or famous. I did it because I had something to say and it seemed like a good opportunity to say it, and I wasn't going to let that opportunity pass. For the first few months after I came out to the media I was making a comment or giving an interview just about every week. Even now I still have journalists calling me up whenever they need a comment about sexual assault or anything to do with it. I've become the face of rape.

But I've also become somebody other victims seek out, because they need someone to talk to and they know I'll understand. I've had people find me through MySpace, they even come up to me in the street. And that's both a good thing and a bad thing. It's great if I can help other girls and give them a bit of reassurance, but it can be hard sometimes too. Some of the people I meet, even if they don't give me a blow-by-blow account of what happened, you can just sense how crushed they are by what's happened to them, and that can be a lot to take on board when you're just walking down the street or hanging out at the pub.

The thing I've realised about rape is that there is no objective way to assess the degree of trauma that victims are going to suffer. It's not the actual assault that determines how bad you're going to feel afterwards, it's how you react to it. Even though I was gang-raped, my reaction hasn't been, 'I'm never going to recover from this.' Whereas someone else might have been the victim of date rape, there might have been no alcohol involved, no betrayal by friends, there might have just been one person, no threat of stabbing, nothing like that, just a simple overpowering – and yet the girl might have been so unable to cope, and suffered so much, that I'd consider the assault worse than mine. So some of the girls I meet really need someone to unload on; others just want to say hello and to tell me that they went through it too and congratulate me on standing up for myself. I'm glad to be able to do that and be there for people, but sometimes it can be an awful lot to take on.

Still, if I'm ever in danger of taking myself too seriously, my friends are always there to put me in my place. I was out recently with my flatmate and a girl came up to me and said, 'Wow, you're Tegan Wagner, aren't you?' And she turned to my flatmate and asked, 'What's it like living with Tegan?'

'She's messy.'

'No, really, really, what's she like?'

'She used dishwashing detergent the other day instead of laundry powder.'

'No no no no, what's she like?'

'An idiot.'

I just cracked up. I may be the face of rape, but I still have to wash my socks and undies.

# 20

# My journey

THIS IS GOING TO sound crazy, but I don't regret what happened to me.

If this had to happen to somebody, I'm glad it happened to me because I was strong enough to take it. Other people might have been completely destroyed by it, but not me. I survived. I'm strong, and I know I'm strong, because I've proved it.

That's not to say it was easy. It was horrible. I was depressed and miserable, suffered anxiety attacks, became bulimic, cut myself, abused drugs to try and escape the trauma. I was a mess. And it didn't just affect me: the rapes put all my relationships – with my grandparents, my mum, my friends – under enormous pressure. A lot of those relationships couldn't take the strain. It made me realise that the only person I could really count on was myself. That's a hard, lonely lesson to learn, especially when you're just a teenager.

I can't imagine what my life would have been like if this hadn't happened to me. Maybe I would have stayed a good little schoolgirl, never getting into any kind of trouble I couldn't talk my way out of. Maybe. All I can do is compare the girl I was before all this happened with the girl I became after it.

Before the rapes, I was loud and boisterous and confident around my friends, but quiet and cautious around other people. As girls, we're taught that the most important thing is to make other people like us, so in group situations we're all so busy being nice we actually do things to hurt our own interests. We let guys take advantage of us, dominate us, bully us, and rape us because we're too afraid to stand up and say, 'You're a creep. I'm out of here.'

After the rapes I began to realise how stupid that was. Why was I worrying so much about other people's feelings? It's not like anyone seemed to be concerned about *my* feelings. I realised being nice doesn't get you anywhere. Being nice just gets you abused. Nowadays, I'm not going to be nice for the sake of being nice. I say what I think, and if that's a problem, tough.

It's hard to let go of that fear of not being liked, the fear of looking stupid in front of other people. Drama helped me let go of that fear. I might have found my way to drama even without being raped – drama's a passion for me, and I think it always would have been. But it gave me the skills and the detachment I needed to walk into the courtroom and stand up to those three stupid fools who were trying to misrepresent me.

When you're the victim in a rape trial, what you're experiencing is an argument about what kind of person you are: whether you're a naïve fourteen-year-old who let herself get drunk and was preyed upon by a group of guys who'd done this before and would do it again in the most ruthless manner. Or whether you're a slutty fourteen-year-old who couldn't wait to offer a sexual smorgasbord to a bunch of guys she'd only just met and whose only concern was that she might get pregnant. That may not be how the lawyers or the judge see it, but that's how I saw it. It was an argument about who Tegan Wagner really was. It was an argument I had to win.

Theatre made going to court every day just about bearable, because it helped me detach myself and stay focused on what the trial process was really about – presenting my case in the best way I could – and not letting myself get so swept up in the emotions that I broke down or started screaming obscenities at the boys or did any of the other things I would have loved to do, but which wouldn't have helped me win.

But we did win. I told my version of the story, and a jury of twelve people agreed that I was telling the truth. There were flaws in the process – I'm still convinced that if the jury had been allowed to give their verdict on Mustapha and Amir, they would have found them guilty, and they would have got much tougher sentences. But overall, I'm happy, because I feel I was vindicated. I spent a lot of years having people tell me I couldn't have been raped, I was lying, I made the whole thing up. Now I've got a judgment in the Supreme Court of New South Wales proving that what I said was true. I *was* raped. I'm not lying. And now the whole world knows it.

There are still a lot of things I'm angry about. Don't get me started on the rights of the accused or the laws of evidence or soft judges or the court calendar or the way the workload's organised at the DPP. Don't get me started on school or bitchy girls or some of my former friends. Don't get me started on some men's attitudes towards women. Just don't. I could go on all day. But the truth is, in spite of all that, I've moved on. I don't get up in the morning angry at the world. My life's actually pretty good these days. In fact, it's all been pretty good since that day in 2006 when the sentences got handed down and I knew those boys were off to jail for a long time. It was like the sun came out.

I was able to move on because I took the power back. I took those boys to court, I saw it through and I stared them down. It really is the best feeling, and that's why I tell every victim to come forward. Do something about it. Take back the power. Make them pay. Because once you have, you can move on.

I know it's not without risks. I would have been devastated if we'd gone to court and lost. But I had the truth on my side. The truth, and evidence, and a fantastic team who weren't going to let the boys get away with it. For me it was worth the risk.

People often ask me how I had the guts to stand up and go public about what happened. For me it was an easy decision to make. I felt like I'd been waiting four years for a chance to speak out, speak my mind. I don't feel ashamed about what happened. I think the boys are the only ones who should feel ashamed. I haven't done anything wrong. I was just in the wrong place at the wrong time. Plus I want to see some good come out of all this, not just for me, but for all the girls like me. By speaking out, I want to encourage other victims to stand up and come forward, to speak out against the shame and the silence. When a girl's been raped, I want people at their school to come up to them and say, 'This happened to someone in my family. I know it's terrible, but you're going to be okay, you're going to get through this.' Not, 'You're ugly, who'd rape you?'

I also want to draw people's attention to the problem of rape in our society. When it happened to me I was so ignorant about rape I almost didn't go to the police because I wasn't sure my experience counted as rape. Schools should be talking about this. As a society we should be talking about this. Both girls and guys need to know what's acceptable and what's not. They need to know what the rules are. And when it happens, they need to know that there's help out there.

Governments need to do more. They need to put more money into rape crisis centres and other support services. The phone counselling services are so understaffed that if you ring up with a problem, you only get to talk for a short period of time before the counsellors have to chuck you off again. There are too many callers, not enough counsellors. Too bad if you need to talk longer than the ten minutes they can offer you.

And most importantly, we need to change the legal system so it's more supportive of the rights of victims. At the moment, everything's tilted in favour of the accused. They get all the care and attention. No one's looking out for the victims. As I was completing this book, the New South Wales government announced plans to change the laws regarding consent, and to change the way sexual assault cases are handled by the legal system. If my experiences, and my decision to speak about them, have helped to make the system a little bit fairer and a bit less traumatic for victims, then that's a fantastic outcome. While there's still a lot more to be done, I'm glad to think the system is changing for the better, and that I had something to do with it.

What happened will always be a part of me. Friends talk to me sometimes about their first sexual experiences and how wonderful they were, and before I can answer, I have to think, okay, forget about your first experience – and your second – and your third. I have to skip onto my fourth experience and pretend it was my first. My first time should have been wonderful – or funny or great or embarrassing or beautiful. Whatever it was, it should have been something I chose. The boys took that first experience away from me and that's something I can never change.

But it does get easier to live with. Days, sometimes weeks will go by and I won't think about it. Then something will happen that'll remind me, and it all comes back. But it happens less and less often, and the pain you feel becomes less intense. You grow past it. You move on.

One night a few weeks ago I got in my car and I drove to the house where the boys used to live. I parked outside and looked at the house. I hadn't been back there since it happened. In all that time, I'd never been back. That night, it was like I was daring myself to look at the thing that scared me the most. And you know what? I didn't feel a thing. No fear, no terror, no anxiety attacks. Nothing. It was just a house. I realised I was finally getting over it.

The boys haven't gone away forever. Mustapha will be out in 2015, Amir in 2016, Sabir in 2026. That's not as far away as it sounds. In my darker moments I wonder whether they're going to get out of jail and come looking for me. But I can't let myself dwell on that. I've got to get on with my life.

I look at my sister now and she's fourteen, going on fifteen, which is exactly how old I was when I was raped. My mum's always telling me how similar we are, my sister and me. We act alike, we look alike. I can't imagine her experiencing what I experienced that night. I can't imagine her even kissing a guy. I can imagine her turning around to her friends and saying, 'Oh my God, he like put his tongue in my mouth, who does that?' But anything more than that? Forget it. I don't know how she'd cope if she had to go through what I went through. She'd probably amaze me, and cope with it, just like I did.

But I hope she never has to.

# Acknowledgements

This book has been a journey for me, one that I have enjoyed but which wouldn't have happened without a few very cool people in the wings.

Mardi McConnochie, the life saver, a big thank you. You put so much effort into the writing process, helping me convert my thoughts into a coherent form.

Paul Sheehan, you got the ball rolling and your support during court and the book's development has been amazing and very much needed, and very much appreciated.

Deb Callaghan and Alex Craig – the two most patient, tolerant and calm people I know, who still manage to smile and have a laugh when I'm late with, or to, something (again!).

And thanks also to my editor, Karen Penning, for getting the book over the line.

I also want to thank Kevin, Tony and Sheridan. These three souls helped me through my court case and have had to put up with me since I was fourteen. Just when they thought they had seen the back of me, I was on the phone grilling them for this project. So here it is guys. Thank you for your amazing support over the years.